MW01173867

Ready Reasons

Ready Reasons

Essays on Christian Apologetics

Daniel J. Yoder

Phroneō Publishing

979-8-9906142-0-8 (Paperback)

979-8-9906142-1-5 (Hardcover)

979-8-9906142-2-2 (E-book)

239 – Apologetics & Polemics

You can send questions, comments, and error reports to dyoder6616@gmail.com. To order additional copies, search for this book on Amazon.

Edited by Jessica N. Yoder.

DEDICATION

To my mom, Donna-Marie.

Your death at a young age left me with few memories of you.

Your refusal to heed an abortion-minded doctor

makes the final essay more personal for me.

TABLE OF CONTENTS

Preface

When I was a teenager, my dad gave me a copy of Josh McDowell's classic work *More Than a Carpenter*. That short book about Jesus introduced me to Christian apologetics – the rational defense of the faith.

In 2015, I had the opportunity to begin teaching at Elnora Bible Institute. After being assigned an introductory apologetics course called *Doubt and Defense*, I enjoyed developing and teaching the class so much I decided to pursue further education in apologetics. This book has emerged from those studies.

In Matthew 22:37, Jesus commands us to love the Lord with every aspect of our nature. That whole-being love for God, according to Jesus, should include our minds. Apologetics is an essential way in which believers can pursue obedience to the "greatest and first commandment" (Matthew 22:38 LEB).

This book is a collection of five Christian apologetics essays you can read in any order. I wrote these essays for a general Christian audience. The intention is for the essays to have enough explanation to be beneficial to readers who are new to the study of Christian apologetics, yet also enough depth to be appreciated by those who are more seasoned in their understanding.

The discussion starters after each essay are intended to facilitate the use of this book in a group study context. The resources in the bibliography could be consulted for further study.

This compilation of essays is not comprehensive in scope. Instead, these five essays provide partial answers to these questions:

How does philosophy contribute to Christian apologetics?
What methodologies can be employed in apologetic encounters?
What is a practical way to start and direct apologetic conversations?
How can Jesus' death and resurrection be discussed with Muslims?
Why should unborn children be regarded as valuable human persons?

I pray that the Lord will use this book to sharpen thinking and spark an ongoing interest in Christian apologetics.

Daniel J. Yoder
Elnora, Indiana
May 8, 2024

Essay One

How Philosophy Applies to Apologetics

Introduction

It has been observed, "To many people, the mention of 'philosophy' brings up an image of gray-haired intellectuals endlessly debating irrelevancies."[1] This could explain why many Christians regard philosophy with a certain amount of caution. They might state that they want to be on guard against "philosophy and empty deceit" (Colossians 2:8 LEB) and "pointless chatter" (2 Timothy 2:16 LEB).

However, in the words of one Christian philosopher: "Our churches are filled with Christians who are idling in intellectual neutral. As Christians, their minds are going to waste."[2] This wasting of minds is likely both a result of and a reason for the lack of interest in philosophy that is demonstrated by many Christians.

---

[1] Vern S. Poythress, "Why Philosophy Matters for Christians," Crossway, October 7, 2014, https://www.crossway.org/articles/why-philosophy-matters-for-christians/ (accessed March 25, 2024).

[2] William Lane Craig, *Reasonable Faith: Christian Truth and Apologetics*, revised edition (Wheaton, IL: Crossway Books, 1994), xiv.

Throughout church history, Christians have held a range of attitudes about the value of studying philosophy. The second-century Christian writer Justin Martyr regarded Christianity as the highest philosophy. In contrast, Tertullian (160-240) thought philosophy had no positive contributions to make to Christianity.[3]

The theologian Augustine (354-430) was willing to use philosophy, although he wanted it to serve his theology. To the medieval theologian Thomas Aquinas (1225-74), the philosophy of Aristotle was a vital tool to use in the defense of the Christian faith. Blaise Pascal (1623-62) wanted to keep Christianity and philosophy distinct.[4]

In light of such diversity of opinion, someone might wonder about the role of philosophy in the thoughtful Christian life. More specifically, how can the study of philosophy contribute to an informed defense of the Christian faith? This essay will offer a thoughtful response to that vital question.

---

[3] H. Lynn Gardner, *Commending and Defending Christian Faith: An Introduction to Christian Apologetics* (Joplin, MO: College Press Publishing Company, 2010), 380.

[4] Gardner, 380.

The Task of Philosophy

C. Stephen Evans cites the definition of philosophy formulated by William James, who described it as "an unusually obstinate effort to think clearly and deeply about fundamental questions."[5]

Philosophers debate the definition of philosophy. For example, some have described it as the activity of significant thinkers throughout history, including the Greek philosophers Socrates, Plato, and Aristotle.[6] Such a description may be another factor in the reluctance of many Christians to engage seriously with philosophy.

Ultimately, philosophy involves thinking through the so-called "Big Questions" of life, such as: Do our lives have meaning? Does it matter how we live? Is there more than this life? Does God exist? Is it possible for us to know anything at all? How are we even supposed to think about answering these questions?[7]

Those questions reflect the topics that fall within the purview of philosophy. Areas of philosophical study

---

[5] As quoted in C. Stephen Evans, *Pocket Dictionary of Apologetics & Philosophy of Religion* (Downers Grove, IL: InterVarsity Press, 2002), 92.

[6] Evans, 92.

[7] Steven B. Cowan and James S. Spiegel, *The Love of Wisdom: A Christian Introduction to Philosophy* (Nashville, TN: B&H Academic, 2009), 1.

include ethics (correct behavior), aesthetics (beauty and taste), logic (correct thinking), epistemology (knowledge), metaphysics (being and reality), and the philosophy of science (an assessment of the processes of scientific inquiry).[8] Adherents of every worldview must engage with these philosophical questions and disciplines.

The Task of Apologetics

The English word *apologetics* is derived from the Greek word *apologia*, which means *defense* or *the act of making a defense*.[9] In 1 Peter 3:15, this word is used to instruct believers about the importance of being ready to "make a defense" (LEB) for their hope. This verse, set in the context of the possibility of suffering for the faith, also explains that believers should demonstrate a gentle and respectful attitude as they defend the faith.[10]

---

[8] An overview of these and other philosophical disciplines is provided in Norman L. Geisler and Paul D. Feinberg, *Introduction to Philosophy: A Christian Perspective* (Grand Rapids, MI: Baker Book House, 1980), 24-37.

[9] William Arndt, Frederick W. Danker, and Walter Bauer, *A Greek-English Lexicon of the New Testament and Other Early Christian Literature* (Chicago: University of Chicago Press, 2000), 117.

[10] Norman L. Geisler, *Baker Encyclopedia of Christian Apologetics* (Grand Rapids, MI: Baker Books, 1999), 37.

Apologetics is "the intellectual defense of the faith."[11] It is "an activity of the Christian mind which attempts to show that the gospel message is true in what it affirms."[12] Relatedly, "an apologist is one who is prepared to defend the [gospel] message against criticism and distortion, and to give evidences of its credibility."[13]

Providing evidence for Christianity is *positive apologetics*. Responding to objections about Christianity and demonstrating the inadequacy of non-Christian worldviews is *negative apologetics*.[14]

Philosophically, apologetics is "the discipline of giving reason or evidence for one's beliefs."[15] If a worldview is irrational, it can reasonably be rejected as inadequate. The rational justification of one's beliefs is not a task for which

---

[11] Timothy R. Phillips and Dennis L. Okholm, *Christian Apologetics in the Postmodern World* (Downers Grove, IL: InterVarsity Press, 1995), 55.

[12] Clark H. Pinnock, "Apologetics," in *New Dictionary of Theology*, edited by Sinclair B. Ferguson and J. I. Packer, (Downers Grove, IL: InterVarsity Press, 2000), 36.

[13] Pinnock, 36.

[14] Tim Barnett, "Why Apologetics?," Stand to Reason, December 26, 2018, https://www.str.org/w/why-apologetics- (accessed April 2, 2024).

[15] Norman L. Geisler and Ronald M. Brooks, *When Skeptics Ask: A Handbook on Christian Evidences*, revised and updated (Grand Rapids, MI: Baker Books, 2013), 317.

only Christians are responsible. Non-Christians must also provide a defense for their beliefs.

The Need for Apologetics

Many reasons have been offered for why apologetics is necessary. Numerous verses provide the basis for Norman Geisler's first point about the need for apologetics: God commands believers to do it. One aspect of the readiness commanded in 1 Peter 3 is an eagerness to share the truth when the opportunity arises. In 2 Corinthians 10:3-5, Paul emphasizes the importance of destroying any argument that is opposed to the knowledge of God. This could include evaluating any philosophical thinking that might hinder a person from entering into a relationship with God.[16]

Paul understood that his ministry involved defending the gospel (Philippians 1:7; 16). Christians must guard against false teaching (Jude 3). Church leaders are to provide sound teaching and refute false teachers (Titus 1:9). God's goal for the defense of the gospel is to lead people into a relationship with himself (2 Timothy 2:24-25).[17]

---

[16] Geisler, *Baker Encyclopedia,* 37.

[17] Geisler, *Baker Encyclopedia,* 37-38.

Geisler's second point about the importance of apologetics relates to human reason. Humans are created in God's image (Genesis 1:27) and are invited to experience Jesus' work of redemption. An aspect of salvation is reflecting the image of God by being renewed in knowledge (Colossians 3:10). God expects his image-bearers to think (Isaiah 1:18), which includes distinguishing between truth and error (1 John 4:6).[18]

The importance of using our God-given reasoning abilities supports Geisler's assertion that "a fundamental principle of reason is that it should give sufficient grounds for belief. An unjustified belief is just that – unjustified."[19] Nothing is inherently wrong with someone desiring evidence before they make a faith decision.

An additional reason for the necessity of apologetics is the intellectual crisis in the modern world, which is demonstrated, for one example, by the fact that many people deny the existence of absolute truth. There is also a more profound problem: humankind's spiritual crisis. People need to hear and accept the gospel message that

---

[18] Geisler, *Baker Encyclopedia*, 38.

[19] Geisler, *Baker Encyclopedia*, 38.

explains the problem of their sin and the solution that is provided by the work of Jesus.[20]

A defense of the Christian faith should be offered in a way that respects the questioner as a person. Christian apologists are to direct their message to people as human beings, not merely as human brains.[21] Their ultimate goal should be to lead people to believe in Jesus. Because ideas matter, Christians must defend their faith by answering skeptics, challenging non-Christian worldviews, and establishing Christianity's plausibility and credibility.

Although the Christian faith must be defended from an intellectual perspective, the preacher Charles Spurgeon wanted Christians to remember that "all the hope of our ministry lies in the Spirit of God operating upon the spirits of men."[22] The Christian apologist must remember that his knowledge and wisdom are not the ultimate determining factors in the fruitfulness of his ministry. The Holy Spirit must work in human hearts for people to come to faith.

---

[20] Peter Kreeft and Ronald K. Tacelli, *Handbook of Christian Apologetics: Hundreds of Answers to Crucial Questions* (Westmont, IL: IVP Academic, 1994), 24.

[21] Phillips and Okholm, 55.

[22] Charles H. Spurgeon, "The Wedding Was Furnished with Guests," in *The Metropolitan Tabernacle Pulpit Sermons*, volume 34 (London: Passmore & Alabaster, 1888), 260.

A Christian View of Philosophy

In Colossians 2:8, Paul offers a warning about philosophy. As S. R. Obitts notes, "Such a warning was to be expected in light of what passed for philosophy in Paul's time."[23] Yet Paul then proceeds to make several philosophical assertions in the following verses, referring to Jesus' deity, bodily form, and headship over all powers and authorities. Those comments would have interested the philosophers of that day. While Paul was not opposed to all philosophical reflection,[24] his thinking was rooted in Jesus, not in "human tradition" or "the elemental spirits of the world" (LEB).

Throughout the Middle Ages, Christian thinkers dominated Western philosophy. More recently, anti-Christian philosophy has risen to the forefront. Given that reality, it is even more important for Christians to do philosophy well.[25] C. S. Lewis pointed out, "If all the world were Christian, it might not matter if all the world were uneducated."[26] A well-reasoned defense of the faith would not be necessary in such

---

[23] S. R. Obitts, "Philosophy, Christian View of," in *Evangelical Dictionary of Theology, Second Edition,* edited by Walter A. Elwell (Grand Rapids, MI: Baker Academic, 2001), 920.

[24] Obitts, 920.

[25] Obitts, 920-21.

[26] C. S. Lewis, *The Weight of Glory: And Other Addresses* (New York: HarperOne, 2001), 58.

a context, but because the church encounters hostility, believers should not expect to be able to get away with sloppy philosophical thinking.

Lewis emphasized the importance of Christians being able to offer intellectual responses to their opponents. He asserted, "Good philosophy must exist, if for no other reason, because bad philosophy needs to be answered."[27] Given Jesus' emphasis on a whole-being love for the Lord (which includes the use of the mind), there is no justification for philosophical ignorance.

It is possible to study philosophy from a Christian perspective. According to Obitts, the first step of the Christian approach to philosophy is to "critically [. . .] scrutinize the discoveries, insights, and theories that have increased our knowledge of God's universe."[28] The second step is to "coherently [. . .] weave this knowledge into an adequate whole consistent with Scripture."[29] A Christian philosopher evaluates all areas of human knowledge from the perspective of the Bible.

In Colossians 2:8, Paul provides three parallel characteristics of the "philosophy and empty deceit" (LEB)

---

[27] Lewis, *The Weight of Glory*, 58.

[28] Obitts, 921.

[29] Obitts, 921.

that Christians are to avoid: that which is "according to human tradition, according to the elemental spirits of the world and not according to Christ" (LEB). God's revelation finds its climactic expression in the person of Jesus Christ.

Philosophy that does not submit to God's revelation takes people *captive*, as numerous translations render Paul's warning. Greg Bahnsen states, "Any line of thinking that does not begin with Christ can end only in foolishness."[30] That is the danger of non-Christian philosophy, which is why Christians must practice philosophy for the glory of God.

The Role of Philosophy in Apologetics

Every worldview makes philosophical assertions. For example, every worldview takes some position about the nature of ultimate reality (the topic of metaphysics). Therefore, apologetics is a vital aspect of Christian thinking because it is "the vindication of the Christian philosophy of life against the various forms of the non-Christian philosophy of life."[31]

---

[30] Greg L. Bahnsen, *Presuppositional Apologetics: Stated and Defended*, edited by Joel McDurmon (Powder Springs, GA; Nacogdoches, TX: American Vision; Covenant Media Press, 2008), 32.

[31] Cornelius Van Til, *Christian Apologetics*, edited by William Edgar, second edition (P&R Publishing Company: Phillipsburg, NJ, 2003), 1.

Two significant aspects of the role of philosophy in apologetics are to evaluate non-Christian worldviews and to defend the Christian worldview. In preparation for that, the words of Douglas Groothuis are appropriate: "Apologetics means philosophical engagement, and philosophy trades on logic. Therefore, a brief discussion of basic logical principles is imperative."[32]

There are three primary laws of logic. These laws of thought are fundamental to all sound thinking and effective communication. The law of non-contradiction is that "no proposition can be both true and false at the same time and in the same sense."[33] Put another way, contradictory statements cannot both be true at the same time. Of course, a particular statement could be true at one time and a contradictory statement could be true at another time.

For example, a statement such as "It is raining" is true when it is raining. The statement "It is not raining" would become true when the rain stops. It is also possible for seemingly contradictory statements to both be true at the same time as long as they are not both true in the same sense. To illustrate, the historic Christian understanding of

---

[32] Douglas Groothuis, *Christian Apologetics: A Comprehensive Case for Biblical Faith* (Downers Grove, IL; Nottingham, England: IVP Academic; Apollos, 2011), 45.

[33] Cowan and Spiegel, 18.

the doctrine of the Trinity is that God is both one and three. That is not a contradiction because God's one-ness relates to his nature, and his three-ness relates to his persons. God can be one and three simultaneously because he is not one and three in the same sense.

According to the law of the excluded middle, "every proposition must be either true or false."[34] As the name indicates, this law excludes the existence of a third possibility. For example, someone either exists or does not exist. There is no third option. No state of partial existence constitutes an alternative to existence and non-existence.

The third fundamental law of logic is the law of identity, which is the idea that "every proposition is identical to itself [. . .] put another way, if a proposition is true, then it is true."[35] This law may seem exceedingly obvious, but it is actually the most basic law of thought. Geisler illustrates this by pointing out that, without the law of identity, the statements "I am I" and "I am a chair" would have no meaningful distinction.[36] It is vital to have a basic understanding of the laws of logic before engaging in

---

[34] Cowan and Spiegel, 18.

[35] Cowan and Spiegel, 18-19.

[36] Geisler, *Baker Encyclopedia*, 427.

worldview evaluation. If a worldview is irrational, it is unworthy of belief.

Evaluation of Non-Christian Worldviews

The crucial ultimate question is, "What is ultimate reality?"[37] The seven major worldviews – atheism, polytheism, panentheism, finite godism, pantheism, deism, and theism – offer a range of answers to that question.

Concerning the nature of ultimate reality, atheism maintains that there is no God; polytheism accepts the existence of many finite gods. The other worldviews believe there is one God but disagree on whether God is finite or infinite. In panentheism, a finite god is identified with the world; in finite godism, a finite god is not identified with the world. In pantheism, an infinite God is identified with the world. Deism and theism both hold to an infinite God who is not identified with the world. In deism, God does not perform miracles. In theism, God does perform miracles.[38]

Regarding these worldviews, "the central premises of each are opposed by the others. That means that logically

---

[37] Garry R. Morgan, *Understanding World Religions in 15 Minutes a Day* (Minneapolis, MN: Bethany House Publishers, 2012), 15.

[38] Norman L. Geisler and William D. Watkins, *Worlds Apart: A Handbook on World Views*, second edition (Grand Rapids, MI: Baker Book House, 1989), 15-16.

only one world view can be true; the others must be false."[39] The three basic laws of logic justify that conclusion. Pantheism is an example of a worldview that is willing to embrace contradictions. Such a level of irrationality is a fatal mark against it.[40]

A logical evaluation of these worldviews demonstrates a necessary function of philosophy in the task of apologetics. Because Christianity is a theistic worldview, Christian theism will be defended later in this essay.

Atheism. Frank Turek regards the so-called *problem of evil* as the most potent argument used in support of atheism. However, his evaluation of that problem leads to a surprising conclusion.[41] The basic idea behind the problem of evil is that if there is an all-powerful and all-loving God (such as the one Christians believe in), there should not be evil in the world. As some atheists express it, since there is evil in the world, the Christian God must be lacking in either power or love. The atheistic idea is that the existence of evil disproves the existence of God.

---

[39] Geisler and Watkins, 15.

[40] Geisler and Watkins, footnote 6 (page 15).

[41] Frank Turek, *Stealing from God: Why Atheists Need God to Make Their Case* (Colorado Springs, CO: NavPress, 2014), 115.

Every worldview is obligated to provide some explanation for the existence of evil. Some worldviews (such as pantheism) claim that evil is an illusion.[42] However, theists acknowledge the existence of evil in the world. They should, therefore, offer a reasonable explanation for how evil can be understood within the Christian worldview.

Atheists are inconsistent on this point. They essentially view evil as an illusion when they posit that people simply "dance to the music"[43] of their DNA. Yet atheists also react to what they perceive to be evil. Logically, atheists should be required to make up their minds on this issue. If their worldview is true, any judgment of a behavior is nothing more than an expression of personal preference. Atheists have no logical grounds for objecting to anything that seems to be evil.[44]

It is important to emphasize that evil, while real, can only exist as a privation, as a deficiency of something good. Evil is a negation of good. For example, someone might describe an action as unjust, in clear contrast to what is just. Without good, a person could not recognize evil. Without God, there could be no good because God provides the

---

[42] Turek, 116.

[43] Turek, 116.

[44] Turek, 116.

perfect standard of what is good. There cannot be objective evil without objective good. There can only be objective good if God exists.[45]

The reality of evil actually provides evidence for the existence of God. As Turek illustrates, "The shadows prove the sunshine."[46] It is possible to have sunshine (good) without shadows (evil), but it is not possible to have shadows without sunshine. As it turns out, the strongest argument against theism in the atheist's arsenal disproves the atheistic worldview.[47]

When Lewis reflected on his time as an atheist, he realized that his objections against the Christian God were grounded in the existence of evil in the universe. He later wrote, "But how had I got this idea of *just* and *unjust?* A man does not call a line crooked unless he has some idea of a straight line. What was I comparing this universe with when I called it unjust?"[48]

Lewis recognized that if he embraced a subjective view of evil rather than an objective view, his argument

---

[45] Turek, 117.

[46] Turek, 117.

[47] Turek, 117-18.

[48] C. S. Lewis, *Mere Christianity* (New York: HarperOne, 2001), 38.

against God's existence would collapse. He realized that he needed to assume the existence of God to argue against God. Without light, someone could never know that something is dark.[49]

Peter Kreeft offers a unique argument. If atheism is true, then there is no Creator. Without a Creator, evolution would be the only option to explain the universe's origin. If there is not a Beginner, there could not be a beginning. Without a beginning or a first cause, the universe must be eternal, meaning that it has been evolving for an infinite amount of time. But how could something evolve for an endless amount of time and yet not be perfect? The process of evolution should be complete. By now, evil should be eradicated.[50]

The claim here is not that atheists actually believe in an eternal universe. Instead, the assertion is that there could not be a beginning without a Beginner. Logically, atheists should believe in an eternal universe, although many do not. Additionally, without a Beginner, some sort of evolutionary process must have occurred. So why is the world not perfectly evolved yet, since the process of evolution must

---

[49] Lewis, *Mere Christianity*, 38-39.

[50] Drawn from an interview recorded in Lee Strobel, *The Case for Faith: A Journalist Investigates the Toughest Objections to Christianity* (Grand Rapids, MI: Zondervan, 2000), 35.

have been going on forever? This line of reasoning is a devastating blow to the atheistic worldview.

Polytheism. The polytheistic acceptance of multiple finite gods is logically problematic. Those gods must be finite because it is logically impossible to have multiple infinite beings. Since the gods are finite, they must be created beings, which means they are dependent and not ultimate beings. For example, if these gods were birthed by nature, then nature is ultimate. Because finite gods cannot be ultimate beings, it is irrational to worship them.[51]

In polytheism, the gods are within the universe. Since there is evidence that the universe is not eternal but came into existence at some point,[52] the conclusion must be that the gods are not eternal. Geisler offers this evaluation: "But if they came into existence, then they are not gods but creatures made by some eternal Cause (God). But if the gods of polytheism derive their existence from another, then this other is really the supreme God of monotheism."[53]

Logically, polytheism leads to monotheism. Imperfect, finite gods imply a perfect, infinite Creator. Polytheism also appears to be a human invention, as

---

[51] Geisler, *Baker Encyclopedia*, 605.

[52] Geisler, *Baker Encyclopedia*, 276-77.

[53] Geisler, *Baker Encyclopedia*, 606.

evidenced by the fact that the gods often reflect the image of humans.[54]

Panentheism. In panentheism, "God is to the world as a soul is to a body."[55] In one sense, God is beyond the world; in another sense, God is the world. In this view, God changes as the world changes. Essentially, God has two poles, one which is unchanging (his actuality) and one which is changing (his potentiality). As one of God's poles, the world is how his potentiality becomes actualized.[56]

Panentheism does not require a Creator but rather a being that animates the world and can be a *world-soul*. It is reasonable to ask, "Why does that being exist rather than not exist?" If God must be referenced in answer to that question, God and the world cannot be codependent. Panentheism claims codependence, but there is no codependence if God is the Creator. Instead, the world would ultimately be entirely dependent on God.[57]

Another dilemma for panentheism relates to the order in which the poles came. "If the potential pole came

---

[54] Geisler, *Baker Encyclopedia*, 606.

[55] Geisler and Feinberg, 433.

[56] Geisler and Brooks, 42.

[57] Kreeft and Tacelli, 95.

before the actual, then how was anything ever actualized? The actual pole could not have come first, because it had no potential to become."[58] They could not always have simultaneously existed because time does not go back into the past forever.[59] There must be an ultimate Creator.

A significant idea in panentheism is that everything, including God, is changing. But how can that be known unless there is some unchanging standard? Change can only be measured if there is a standard. Panentheism has no rational basis for the claim that all is changing.[60] Like polytheism, panentheism leads logically to monotheism because only monotheism provides an unchanging standard.

Finite Godism. One major problem for finite godism is that a finite god needs a Creator. Perhaps the finite god is a great created being, but he is created nevertheless. This is consistent with the law of causality (the idea that all finite beings require a cause). A god who is caused cannot be regarded as the ultimate reality. Instead, that finite god's Creator would be the ultimate reality. A finite, created god is not worthy of worship or any expression of ultimate commitment. Furthermore, because

---

[58] Geisler and Brooks, 45.

[59] Geisler, *Baker Encyclopedia*, 277.

[60] Geisler and Brooks, 45.

a finite god is necessarily limited, it does not qualify as a standard of absolute goodness. A finite being cannot be infinitely good. Therefore, the being who, in reality, possesses absolute goodness must be an infinite God.[61]

Pantheism. Like atheism, pantheism encounters a significant challenge with evil. The pantheistic worldview portrays evil as an illusion. However, labeling it an illusion is unsatisfying to anyone who has had a personal experience with evil. A more profound issue relates to the origin of the illusion. If evil is an illusion, why does everyone have the same illusion? If evil is an illusion, what is the source of the illusion? If evil is an illusion, why does it seem so real?[62] Those questions have no logically satisfactory answers.

Additionally, pantheism cannot ultimately even admit an absolute good because, in this view, "The ground of all is beyond being and knowing. It is beyond the laws of logic and distinction."[63] If God is beyond both good and evil, then there is no basis for distinguishing between good and evil.

---

[61] Geisler and Watkins, 211-14.

[62] Norman L. Geisler, *Christian Apologetics* (Grand Rapids: Baker Book House, 1976), 189.

[63] Geisler, *Christian Apologetics*, 189.

Deism. Deists believe that there is a God who created the universe, but they deny that God performs miracles. However, a being that brought the universe into existence could also perform other miracles. As Geisler puts it, "It seems self-defeating to admit a great miracle like creation and then to deny the possibility of lesser miracles."[64] That is a substantial problem for deists.

The laws of nature are general and descriptive, not universal and prescriptive. If something is descriptive, it describes what is the case. If something is prescriptive, it prescribes what ought to be the case. Because the laws of nature are descriptive, not prescriptive, God can intervene in nature by performing a miracle.[65] He can suspend natural laws without violating his character.

A God who is no longer involved with his creation in any meaningful way appears to have abandoned it. But how can someone completely rule out the option for God to continue to be involved with his created world? The deistic rejection of miracles also leads to a rejection of supernatural revelation. However, is there a good reason for rejecting the possibility of God providing supernatural revelation? If creation is granted, the possibility of God's

---

[64] Geisler, *Baker Encyclopedia*, 191.

[65] Geisler, *Baker Encyclopedia*, 191.

ongoing involvement with the world by way of both miracles and revelation must also be acknowledged.[66]

Defense of the Christian Worldview

Gary Crampton declares, "After demonstrating the internal incoherence of [. . .] non-Christian views," the Christian apologist "will show how Christianity is self-consistent."[67] Part of that task includes demonstrating how Christianity "answers questions and solves problems that other worldviews cannot."[68]

How do non-Christian worldviews fare when subjected to philosophical analysis? The previous section noted that the problem of evil disproves atheism. Polytheism appears to be a human invention. It could only be possible if a theistic God created the many gods, but in that case, the worldview collapses. Panentheism also cannot avoid an infinite Creator. Finite godism encounters the same problem. Pantheism can only offer a philosophically unsatisfying explanation for evil in the world. Deism lacks

---

[66] Geisler, *Baker Encyclopedia*, 191-92.

[67] As quoted in Doug J. Douma, *The Presbyterian Philosopher: The Authorized Biography of Gordon H. Clark* (Eugene, OR: Wipf and Stock, 2016), 105.

[68] Gary Crampton, as quoted in Douma, 105.

logical coherence. In light of that analysis, theism appears to be the only remaining option.

The theistic worldview is not limited to Christianity. Islam and Judaism are two other theistic worldviews. Making a complete case for the Christian worldview over Islam and Judaism would require a detailed analysis of topics such as the evidence for the reliability of the New Testament, the deity of Jesus, and the resurrection of Jesus. Such a case will not be pursued here, but that evidence does present a strong argument for the Christian version of the theistic worldview.

In this essay, a logical defense of the Christian worldview will be offered. A necessary test of any worldview is how it makes sense of the external world:

- Is there anything about the biblical worldview that is inconsistent with the world around us?
- Does the biblical worldview explain the universe's existence, origin, and sustenance?
- Do its adherents need to devise a creative way to explain away miracles?
- Does it explain human intelligence and consciousness?
- Does the biblical worldview explain why there is evil in the world?
- Does it explain why evil seems to be wrong?

- Does it give hope for the eventual defeat of evil?

- Does the biblical worldview explain the notion of morality?

- Does it explain the human ability to engage in philosophical reflection?

Jason Lisle emphasizes that a worldview must provide what he calls "preconditions of intelligibility."[69] These preconditions "must be accepted as true before we can know anything about the universe."[70] Examples include the accuracy of human memory, the reliability of human senses, and the laws of logic. Many people take these preconditions for granted, but every worldview must explain why they are often taken for granted.[71] The fact that they are typically assumed is not in and of itself an adequate explanation for their origin. To focus on the laws of thought in particular, Lisle states, "Rational reasoning involves using the laws of logic. Therefore, a rational worldview must be able to account for the existence of such laws."[72]

---

[69] Jason Lisle, *The Ultimate Proof of Creation: Resolving the Origins Debate* (Green Forest, AR: Master Books), 38.

[70] Lisle, 38.

[71] Lisle, 38-39.

[72] Lisle, 51.

The laws of logic should seem obvious to any rational person, but why are they true? The Christian God is the ultimate standard who provides a basis for reasoning.

The law of non-contradiction reflects how God thinks – he is perfectly rational and, therefore, cannot contradict himself. The laws of logic are grounded in God's nature. Only the Christian worldview provides a foundation for the laws of logic.[73] By contrast, atheism cannot account for any of the preconditions of intelligibility. Because there is no aspect of the external world that cannot be accounted for in the Christian worldview, critics must provide a reasonable counter-explanation for the world in which humans find themselves.

As Lewis, a former atheist, realized, "Supposing there was no intelligence behind the universe, no creative mind. In that case nobody designed my brain for the purpose of thinking."[74]

He correctly realized that there is only one reasonable implication to draw: "Unless I believe in God, I

---

[73] Lisle, 51-52.

[74] C. S. Lewis, as quoted in Justin Brierley, *The Surprising Rebirth of Belief in God: Why New Atheism Grew Old and Secular Thinkers Are Considering Christianity Again* (Carol Stream, IL: Tyndale Elevate, 2023), 181.

can't believe in thought: so I can never use thought to disbelieve in God."[75]

If Lewis and Lisle are correct, then philosophy is only possible because Christianity is true. If the existence of philosophy proves that Christianity is true, that is a powerful apologetic argument.

Conclusion

As Groothuis clarifies, apologetics "walks arm in arm with philosophy."[76] His definition of philosophy is "the investigation of significant truth claims through rational analysis."[77] Philosophy and apologetics are connected because Christian apologists must be able to present a rationally compelling case for Christianity.

Two major apologetics-related tasks are the evaluation of non-Christian worldviews and the defense of the Christian worldview. Those tasks cannot be done effectively without a philosophical foundation.

---

[75] C. S. Lewis, as quoted in Brierley, 181.

[76] Groothuis, 27.

[77] Groothuis, 27.

Discussion Starters

1. Before reading this essay, how well did you understand the concept of philosophy? If you thought of philosophy as either dangerous or valuable, why?

2. Do you agree that doing philosophy from a Christian perspective is possible? Why or why not?

3. Before reading this essay, how well did you understand the concept of Christian apologetics? How would you explain how philosophy can contribute to apologetics?

4. Have you ever had a worldview discussion with someone who held a different worldview than you? What did you learn from that? How has this essay equipped you to evaluate other worldviews logically?

Essay Two
A Dialogical Approach to Apologetics

Introduction

Imagine asking an experienced carpenter to identify his favorite tool. He might point to his trusty twenty-ounce straight claw hammer. As he has swung the hammer many thousands of times over the years, it has come to feel like an extension of himself. It fits nicely into his hand, and he enjoys using it. He cannot imagine showing up at a job site without his hammer.

Even if that hammer is the carpenter's favorite tool, should it be the only tool in his toolbox? It certainly has its place; it is the best tool for driving a framing nail. But what if he needs to measure a window or rip a piece of plywood? Despite how much he likes his hammer, there may be times when a specific job requires using a different tool.

An analogy can be drawn between the work of a carpenter and the work of an apologist. The dialogical approach gives the apologist the flexibility to employ a variety of apologetic methodologies.

To most benefit from this essay, the reader must understand what apologetics is and why it is necessary. Those concepts are explained on pages 4-8 of this book.

Dialogical Apologetics

Defining Dialogical Apologetics. Apologists have taken different approaches to the task of defending the Christian faith. An apologist may have a favorite approach that he is always willing and able to use. However, there may be times when a different approach is more appropriate. The different apologetic approaches could be likened to tools in the toolbox of the apologist.

The dialogical apologetic methodology is consistent with the fact that there is not a one-size-fits-all approach to the apologetic task. Because various techniques could be employed, a wise apologist will select the approach best-suited to the specific encounter. Edward Carnell observed, "Since apologetics is an art and not a science, there is no 'official' way to defend the Christian faith."[1]

David Clark is credited with developing the dialogical apologetic methodology. Phil Fernandes provides a summary of six significant aspects of this approach. First,

---

[1] As quoted in Kenneth Boa and Robert M. Bowman Jr., *Faith Has Its Reasons: Integrative Approaches to Defending the Christian Faith* (Westmont, IL: IVP Books, 2012), 438.

it is person-centered in that it recognizes that every individual is unique and should be treated as such. An apologetic approach that is effective with one person might not be effective with another person. Different techniques and arguments may need to be used depending on the situation. As Fernandes states, "We should care enough about the person with whom we are dialoguing to get to know them and the way they think."[2]

Second, the dialogical approach is flexible. It involves a willingness to use various arguments for the Christian worldview. A cumulative case can be built by appealing to different arguments and evidence. The apologist does not need to "put all his eggs in one basket."[3]

Third, it does not require Christianity to be proven with logical necessity. Instead, the dialogical apologist seeks to establish the probability of Christianity compared to other worldviews. Rational certainty can be attained in mathematics, for example, but not in such areas as evaluating worldviews. Given that fact, there is a need for humility in the use of reason.[4]

---

[2] Phil Fernandes, *The Fernandes Guide to Apologetic Methodologies* (Ottawa, ON: True Freedom Press, 2024), 199.

[3] Fernandes, 199.

[4] Fernandes, 199-200.

Fourth, the dialogical apologist is willing to use different apologetic methodologies. In particular, this essay will consider the contributions made by evidential apologetics, classical apologetics, testimonial apologetics, presuppositionalism, scientific apologetics, and comparative religious apologetics. The dialogical apologist is willing to "become all things to all men" to lead some to Jesus (see 1 Corinthians 9:19-23). There is no need to limit oneself to a single method in defense of the faith.[5]

Fifth, the dialogical apologist regards theism (belief in a personal God) as an explanation of reality that is more plausible than rival worldviews. Sixth, the dialogical apologist seeks to demonstrate the logical consistency of the Christian worldview. The Christian worldview is a credible explanation of reality and is internally consistent.[6]

The Rationale for Dialogical Apologetics. David Clark says, "Apologetics has traditionally centered on the philosophical to the exclusion of the personal."[7] In contrast, the dialogical approach is personal. It is valuable

---

[5] Fernandes, 200.

[6] Fernandes, 200.

[7] David K. Clark, *Dialogical Apologetics: A Person-Centered Approach to Christian Defense* (Grand Rapids, MI: Baker Books, 1993), viii.

because it does not divorce the task of apologetics from the real-life situations people encounter.

This approach does not discount the importance of philosophical or intellectual matters. Still, it is a reminder that those cognitive activities should not be permanently disconnected from life. A fact to be remembered is that "every assessment of the case for Christianity is made by real people who have unique agendas firmly in place."[8] The uniqueness of people requires an audience-centered approach. The dialogical approach "is unique in recognizing the variety of ways in which real people will evaluate apologetic arguments."[9]

Many apologetic approaches are results-oriented. With that mindset, the goal of an apologetic encounter is to bring an unbeliever to faith. Without diminishing the importance of that goal, dialogical apologetics is not focused on mere results. Instead, there is an appreciation of the value of honest dialogue and genuine relationships. This is an audience-focused, not a result-focused, approach.[10]

Max Warren suggested that "'Dialogue' is not evangelism [. . .] It is an activity in its own right. It is in its

---

[8] Clark, viii.

[9] Clark, ix.

[10] Clark, 102-03.

very essence an attempt at mutual 'listening,' listening in order to understand. Understanding is its reward."[11]

The quality of a conversation does not need to hinge on the extent of agreement that is reached. Instead, "success in dialogue is presenting the case for Christianity, by the Spirit's power, with rational force, cultural appropriateness, and personal sensitivity in the context of relationship."[12]

This methodology "recognizes both strengths and weaknesses in other traditional apologetic approaches."[13] Those other approaches have their place, but it could be noted that "each also exaggerates its strong points in relation to other facets of a balanced apologetic."[14]

The dialogical approach developed by David Clark incorporated the unique strengths of these four approaches: existential apologetics, presuppositional apologetics, evidential apologetics, and classical apologetics. He did not regard his method as a fifth approach but as another class of approach, being person-centered rather than content-

---

[11] As quoted in John Stott, *The Preacher's Notebook: The Collected Quotes, Illustrations, and Prayers of John Stott*, edited by Mark Meynell (Bellingham, WA: Lexham Press, 2018), chapter 3, under "Tolerance," Logos Bible Software Research Edition.

[12] Clark, 122.

[13] Clark, 103.

[14] Clark, 103.

centered. The person-centered approach relates to both practice and theory.[15]

This essay does not follow David Clark's approach, although it shares his understanding of the apologist's goal. He stated that his goal as an apologist is "to present the best case I can for the truth as I see it for the benefit of others."[16]

Illustrating Dialogical Apologetics. The book of Acts provides several illustrations of an audience-centered approach. In Acts 2:14-41, Peter preached a sermon on the day of Pentecost to a Jewish audience. He used three primary arguments to argue that Jesus is the Jewish Messiah: Jesus' miracles (v. 22), Jesus' fulfillment of prophecy (vv. 25-31), and Jesus' resurrection (v. 32).[17]

Jesus' miracles commended him as someone whom God had sent, as Nicodemus acknowledged in John 3:2. The term *attested* was used by Peter to refer to Jesus' holding of an official office (Acts 2:22 LEB). Kenneth Gangel explains, "Jesus' mighty acts pointed to divine power

---

[15] Clark, 103-10.

[16] Clark, 122.

[17] William Lane Craig, *On Guard: Defending Your Faith with Reason and Precision* (Colorado Springs, CO: David C Cook, 2010), 15.

behind his life and ministry, thereby certifying that he was the Messiah."[18]

Peter crafted his approach for his Jewish audience. He identified numerous pieces of evidence for Jesus' resurrection, including the tomb of David in Jerusalem, the eyewitnesses, the Holy Spirit who was poured out on the disciples that day, and the ascension (which the disciples witnessed). He appealed to Psalm 16:8-11, a messianic prophecy that predicts Jesus' resurrection.[19]

A noteworthy challenge facing the Christian apologist is that many people in today's world do not have an understanding of concepts such as sin and salvation. In addressing the Jews, Peter knew that his audience was anticipating the coming of the Messiah, so he could focus on the arguments for why Jesus fit the criteria for the Messiah.[20]

A contrast could be drawn with Acts 17:22-31, which recounts how Paul addressed a Gentile (non-Jewish)

---

[18] Kenneth O. Gangel, *Acts*, volume 5, Holman New Testament Commentary (Nashville, TN: Broadman & Holman, 1998), 28.

[19] Gangel, 28-29.

[20] Nancy Pearcey, "Foreword," in Gregory Koukl, *The Story of Reality: How the World Began, How It Ends, and Everything Important That Happens in Between* (Grand Rapids, MI: Zondervan, 2017), 13-14.

audience in Athens. Paul began at a more foundational level than Peter did because his audience did not have background knowledge of the Hebrew Scriptures. Paul started by presenting God as the Creator. That is consistent with his approach with a Gentile audience in Lystra (Acts 14:15-17). Paul stated that, through the created world, God "did not leave himself without witness" (LEB).[21]

In Acts 17, Paul argued that the God he was proclaiming to the Epicurean and Stoic philosophers is the God who made the world. The city of Athens was permeated with idols, and Paul sought to emphasize that he was speaking about a self-existent and self-sufficient God. Having begun with creation, he argued that the Creator desires a relationship with people.[22]

Paul quoted from several well-known Greek poets. Their affirmation that humans are God's offspring means that, because humans are personal beings, God must also be a personal being. Because the cause must be at least equal to the effect, human life could not have a lifeless idol as its source.[23]

---

[21] Pearcey, 14.

[22] Pearcey, 14.

[23] Pearcey, 14-15.

Having laid that foundation, Paul moved to the moral implications of his message. Being created as personal beings by a personal God makes it logical to conclude that God seeks a relationship with people. Humans are obligated to honor the God who created them. Humanity's failure to honor God is an ethical breach for which people are to repent. At this point, Paul refers to Jesus, whose status as Savior and Judge is confirmed by the resurrection.[24]

After explaining the progression of Paul's discourse, Nancy Pearcey writes, "Evangelicals often put things backward, seeking to persuade people of their sin when they have no idea yet what the term means."[25] It should be no surprise that "the typical response to their message is, 'Don't call me a sinner! Why do I owe this God anything? Besides, I'm not even sure God exists.'"[26] These examples demonstrate the importance of approaching an apologetic encounter in a way that addresses the audience's needs. The apologist's starting point should be determined by the audience. The message of the gospel does not change; the method used to present the gospel often should change.

---

[24] Pearcey, 15.

[25] Pearcey, 15.

[26] Pearcey, 15.

The Role of Evidential Apologetics

Defining Evidential Apologetics. The evidential approach to apologetics emphasizes rational arguments and evidence. The evidential apologist holds to three main ideas. First, there is a recognition that humans were created with the ability to reason. As rational beings, humans should seek to believe what is true. Second, there is a recognition that profound intellectual objections have been raised against the Christian faith. Those objections merit thoughtful and reasonable responses.[27]

Third, there is an acknowledgment that rational arguments and evidence can help lead people to faith as they are given answers to their objections. For example, logical arguments were instrumental in C. S. Lewis' journey to faith. Some evidentialists consider it irrational to accept a belief that is not based on rational arguments. All evidentialists consider rational arguments to have value. Still, they do not all view arguments as necessary for having faith in God. Even though all evidentialists use evidence, they do not all use it the same way.[28]

---

[27] James K. Beilby, "Varieties of Apologetics," in *Christian Apologetics: An Anthology of Primary Sources*, edited by Khaldoun A. Sweis and Chad V. Meister (Grand Rapids, MI: Zondervan, 2012), 32.

[28] Beilby, 32.

The prominent evidential apologist Gary Habermas "tends to focus chiefly on the legitimacy of accumulating various historical evidences for the truth of Christianity."[29] Josh McDowell is another notable example. His approach involves presenting historical and archaeological evidence to make the case for the reliability of the Bible, after which he moves into offering proof for Jesus.[30]

A key point McDowell makes is that the 66 books of the Protestant Bible comprise the actual canon of Scripture. He uses different tests to make that case and points out how the extra books in the Roman Catholic Bible fail these tests. He also appeals to fulfilled prophecy and the evidence for Jesus' resurrection. In McDowell's thinking, it is vital to establish the reliability of the New Testament because that helps to establish the historical basis for Christianity.[31]

Strengths of Evidential Apologetics. Habermas thinks this approach can help those who are struggling with their Christian beliefs. He writes, "I contend that evidential arguments can profitably be utilized in strengthening

---

[29] Gary R. Habermas, "Evidential Apologetics," in *Five Views on Apologetics*, edited by Stanley N. Gundry and Steven B. Cowan, Zondervan Counterpoints Collection (Grand Rapids, MI: Zondervan, 2000), 92.

[30] Fernandes, 89.

[31] Fernandes, 89-92.

believers who have questions or even factual doubts."[32] This approach can also be helpful when witnessing to unbelievers because it does not require a person to provide evidence for God's existence before presenting the gospel. That can be useful when the time for a conversation is limited. The fact that evidentialism is a "one-step approach" allows for "a more direct presentation of the gospel by using data that are still very persuasive."[33]

This approach does well to emphasize factual evidence. Apologetics is about defending the truth of Christianity. If truth is understood as "what corresponds to reality," then it makes sense for an apologetic approach to emphasize how Christianity corresponds to reality.[34]

Jesus' resurrection is a historical event and can be studied using the tools of the historian. The Bible is a historical book and can be studied as such. Kenneth Boa and Robert Bowman express the importance of the factual basis of Christianity when they write, "Fact does not force faith, but faith cannot be divorced from fact."[35]

---

[32] Habermas, 121.

[33] Habermas, 121.

[34] Boa and Bowman, 213.

[35] Boa and Bowman, 213.

Weaknesses of Evidential Apologetics. Norman Geisler points out several weaknesses of the evidential approach (which he calls historical apologetics).[36] First, it sometimes operates on the false assumption that the facts *speak for themselves*. Facts are not self-interpreting but rather are understood within the context of a person's worldview. The way someone understands the connection between specific facts depends on their perspective. The historical evidence for Jesus' resurrection will not be understood as pointing to a miracle if a person's worldview rules out the possibility of miracles.

This relates to Geisler's second point, which is that a person will not identify a miracle as "the fingerprint of God"[37] unless they know enough about God to have some sense of what his fingerprints are like. As Geisler puts it: "Only if one knows what God is like can he identify god-like acts. The very identifiability of an unusual act as a miracle depends on prior knowledge of such a God."[38]

Illustrating Evidential Apologetics. In Acts 2, Peter took an evidential approach with his Jewish audience.

---

[36] Norman L. Geisler, *Baker Encyclopedia of Christian Apologetics*, Baker Reference Library (Grand Rapids, MI: Baker Books, 1999), 319-20.

[37] Geisler, 320.

[38] Geisler, 320.

He did not offer philosophical arguments for God's existence because his audience already acknowledged the existence of God. Evidential apologetics is likely to be most effective in two particular contexts. First, it helps respond to questions about Christianity raised by believers. The historical evidence for Christianity can strengthen faith.

Second, it is helpful in apologetic encounters with non-Christians who acknowledge God's existence. Because Jews and Muslims believe in an eternal God who can perform miracles, the apologist can, for example, move immediately into the evidence for Jesus' resurrection. That evidence helps to confirm Jesus' claims about himself. If he was resurrected, it is not unreasonable to respond in faith to his offer of salvation. Evidentialism seems most applicable to those who are theistic in their worldview. As David Clark writes, "Evidential apologetics works well for those who already assume God."[39]

The Role of Classical Apologetics

Defining Classical Apologetics. This apologetic approach is given its name because of its ancient pedigree. It is a two-step methodology that first involves arguing for God's existence and then, second, moves to presenting

---

[39] Clark, 108.

evidence for Christianity specifically. It seeks to establish theism in general and then defend Christianity as the correct theistic worldview. There is a logical progression from arguing that a God exists to arguing that the Christian God exists. Classical apologists think such pieces of evidence for Christianity as fulfilled prophecy and miracles are not persuasive to those who do not affirm God's existence. Suppose a person does not believe that there is a God who can reveal prophecy or act miraculously. In that case, he will never acknowledge any evidence of that God.[40]

Unlike evidentialists, classical apologists maintain it is logically necessary to establish the existence of God (theism) before presenting arguments for the truthfulness of Christianity.[41] Unlike presuppositionalists, classical apologists maintain that the traditional theistic proofs for God (such as the cosmological and teleological arguments) are valid. They might not accept every argument for God's existence. Still, they often accept the validity of some of those arguments.[42]

Some critical pieces of evidence used to argue for the truthfulness of Christianity include Jesus' resurrection and the historical reliability of the New Testament. As Geisler puts it,

---

[40] Beilby, 32.

[41] Beilby, 32-33.

[42] Geisler, 154-55.

"The basic argument of the classical apologist is that it makes no sense to speak about the resurrection as an act of God unless as a logical step it is established that there is a God who can act."[43] Unless there is a God, it is not possible for the Bible to be the Word of God or for Jesus to be the Son of God.[44]

Strengths of Classical Apologetics. First, an important strength of classical apologetics is its concern for questions of truth. This is significant because of the God-given capacity of the human mind to reason and seek to make sense of the world. There is a God-given rational order in the world. Classical apologetics is consistent with humankind's creation in God's image. As image-bearers, humans are uniquely capable of reflecting the rationality of God, although that reflection might be quite dim at times due to the impact of sin on the human mind.[45]

Augustine affirmed the importance of reason: "The image of the creator is to be found in the rational or intellectual soul of humanity [. . .] The human soul has been

---

[43] Geisler, 155.

[44] Geisler, 155.

[45] Alister E. McGrath, *Mere Apologetics: How to Help Seekers and Skeptics Find Faith* (Grand Rapids, MI: Baker Books, 2012), 104.

created according to the image of God [. . .] that it may use reason and intellect [. . .] to apprehend and behold God."[46]

Second, the classical apologist recognizes the importance of logic. Human communication would not be possible apart from the laws of logic. Logic is helpful for evaluating both the arguments of the apologist and the arguments used against the Christian faith. Arguments against Christianity are discredited if they are logically invalid. Christian belief is rational, and logical arguments can demonstrate that fact.[47]

Third, classical apologists recognize that worldviews form an interpretive framework by which people interpret the facts they encounter. This recognition of the importance of worldviews is expressed in this statement: "Classical apologists encourage nontheists to try looking at the world through theistic glasses and see the difference it will make."[48] For example, a discussion between a Christian and an atheist about the possibility of miracles is actually a discussion about whether or not God exists. A person's

---

[46] As quoted in McGrath, 104.

[47] Boa and Bowman, 127-28.

[48] Boa and Bowman, 129.

worldview will always shape the way they approach the topic of miracles.[49]

Weaknesses of Classical Apologetics. David Clark acknowledges the usefulness of clarifying the difference between the defense of theism in general and Christianity in particular. However, he maintains that some classical apologists are too rigid in enforcing that distinction. He thinks "conversants may legitimately wander back and forth between the two stages as they assess the total cumulative weight of the case for Christianity."[50]

Another critique is that classical apologetics places too much confidence in reason.[51] While logical validity is valuable, it also has limitations. Those who refuse to acknowledge the truth will reject sound arguments and solid evidence that point toward the truth.

Illustrating Classical Apologetics. In Acts 17, Paul essentially took a classical apologetic approach with his Greek audience. He refuted their polytheistic idolatry and made a case for the existence of the one true God who is not dependent on humans for his existence or his sustenance. Paul then moved from the case for God to the

---

[49] Boa and Bowman, 129.

[50] Clark, 109.

[51] Clark, 109.

case for Christianity. The concept of sin and God's solution to man's sin through Jesus was the logical conclusion of Paul's prior argumentation. Those points do not make sense apart from a theistic worldview.

The role of classical apologetics seems to be in interactions with non-theists. In particular, atheists will likely require arguments for God before they are willing to engage with the evidence for Jesus' resurrection.

The Role of Testimonial Apologetics

Defining Testimonial Apologetics. Fernandes writes, "Even many Christians who claim to be opposed to apologetics [. . .] actually defend the faith by sharing their testimonies."[52] They, therefore, do apologetics without realizing it. Testimonial apologetics involves pointing to changed lives as evidence for Christianity. It can be used to supplement other methods.[53]

After historical evidence has been offered for Christianity, the apologist might talk about how his life changed after he became a Christian. McDowell's book *More Than a Carpenter* is almost entirely devoted to evidential apologetics, yet the final chapter is entitled "He Changed My

---

[52] Fernandes, 201.

[53] Fernandes, 201.

Life." One change McDowell attributes to Jesus is how he began loving his father, whom he had previously hated.[54]

Strengths of Testimonial Apologetics. One strength of testimonial apologetics is its biblical support. True saving faith will lead to a life change, which can be manifested by good works (James 2:26). In 1 Corinthians 6:11, Paul describes how Christianity transformed those who previously lived unrighteously. Confessing Jesus as Lord must lead to a transformation of life.[55] Another strength of testimonial apologetics is that it has an existential force. Dramatic change in one person's life can have significant persuasive power to others.

Weaknesses of Testimonial Apologetics. One weakness of testimonial apologetics is it cannot stand on its own as an apologetic approach. Fernandes asserts, "Alone, the testimony of transformed lives does not provide an adequate defense of the gospel."[56] For this reason, it is best to use testimonial apologetics in a supplemental role.

A second weakness of testimonial apologetics is its subjective nature. For every experience, there is an equal

---

[54] Josh McDowell and Sean McDowell, *More Than a Carpenter*, revised edition (Carol Stream, IL: Tyndale Momentum, 2009), 159-68.

[55] Fernandes, 202.

[56] Fernandes, 201.

and opposite experience. Life change does not automatically prove heart change. Even when heart change has happened, it does not prove that Jesus did it. Someone's life is likely to change if they become a Muslim. Christians would not accept such a life change as validation for the truthfulness of Islam. People change all the time for all types of reasons, so there are limitations regarding what can be concluded from an experience of life change.

Illustrating Testimonial Apologetics. When testimonial apologetics is practiced, three factors must be present: the transformation must be thorough, genuine, and permanent. The transformation must be reflected in a lasting change in every aspect of a person's life. The testimony of transformation must be presented accurately (without exaggerations or fabrications).[57]

Paul shared his testimony in Acts 22:1-21 and Acts 26:1-23. In both of those instances, he used his testimony to offer a defense of the Christian faith. He testified to how the grace of God had transformed his life. James Montgomery Boice says pointedly, "If you are not testifying to God's grace or if you feel you cannot, you need to examine yourself to see whether you have really met

---

[57] Fernandes, 201.

Jesus."[58] Testimonial apologetics can supplement other approaches by engaging with people who are not looking for intellectual arguments. It might be most effective with those who are longing for a life change.[59]

The Role of Presuppositionalism

Defining Presuppositionalism.

A primary trait of the presuppositional approach to apologetics is an appeal to authority. Presuppositionalists believe the primary problem facing non-Christians is their sinfulness, which is manifested in rebellion against God. Because of the effects of sin, "the authority of Scripture and of Jesus Christ must be presupposed before sense can be made of arguments for the truthfulness of Christianity."[60] In this approach, "there are no argumentative steps that lead directly to the conclusion of the truthfulness of Christianity."[61] Evidence, reasons, and arguments cannot overcome humanity's sin problem.

---

[58] James Montgomery Boice, *Acts: An Expositional Commentary* (Grand Rapids, MI: Baker Books, 1997), 405.

[59] Fernandes, 201.

[60] Beilby, 33.

[61] Beilby, 33.

Early in his career as a philosopher, Gordon Clark held to dogmatic presuppositionalism. In that view, a person must dogmatically presuppose his first principles and then deduce all other knowledge from this starting point. Gordon Clark later held to Scripturalism, the view that truth can only be found in the Bible and reasonable deductions from the Bible.[62] He considered the logical consistency of Christianity to be fundamental for having confidence in its truthfulness.[63]

Cornelius Van Til held to transcendental presuppositionalism. A key component of Van Til's thinking was his argument that the existence of the Triune God should be presupposed because reality is not intelligible otherwise.[64]

Van Til thought that meaning and intelligibility (concepts such as truth, logic, and value) would not be possible unless the biblical God exists. This is not an argument for Christianity directly, but instead, it is a *reductio ad absurdum* of non-Christian worldviews.[65] Reductio ad

---

[62] Fernandes, 147.

[63] Beilby, 34.

[64] Fernandes, 149-151.

[65] Beilby, 33.

absurdum is "a method of proving the falsity of a premise by showing that its logical consequence is absurd or contradictory."[66] If non-Christian worldviews are absurd, the Christian worldview is vindicated. To the presuppositionalist, while a person does not need to believe in God to be logical, logic is only possible because God exists.

Strengths of Presuppositionalism. One strength of presuppositionalism is the emphasis on sin and the impact of sin on minds and hearts. Sin has a blinding effect. Unbelievers cannot be argued into Christianity apart from the transforming work of the Holy Spirit.

Jason Lisle, who takes a presuppositional approach to apologetics, provides an insight that affirms another strength of this approach. He explains that a worldview must provide what he refers to as "preconditions of intelligibility."[67] Lisle's ideas are summarized on pages 26-28 of this book.

Weaknesses of Presuppositionalism. A weakness of presuppositionalism is its underestimation of the power of facts. Facts have apologetic value, as Boa and Bowman state when they write, "The truth is that one valid and

---

[66] Catherine Soanes and Angus Stevenson, eds., *Concise Oxford English Dictionary* (Oxford: Oxford University Press, 2004).

[67] Jason Lisle, *The Ultimate Proof of Creation: Resolving the Origins Debate* (Green Forest, AR: Master Books), 38.

effective way of challenging people's faulty philosophy of fact is to confront them with facts that do not fit their philosophy."[68]

Other apologetic approaches can challenge non-Christians with the evidence for biblical miracles and fulfilled prophecies. Presenting the evidence for an event like Jesus' resurrection "can itself go far to bursting the bubble of non-Christian worldviews."[69] A second weakness of presuppositionalism is that it unnecessarily limits the arguments an apologist can use. A rejection of the traditional theistic arguments is unmerited and needlessly restrictive.

Illustrating Presuppositionalism. Greg Bahnsen finds an illustration of presuppositionalism in Paul's dialogue with the Athenian philosophers in Acts 17. Bahnsen sees similarities between this passage and Romans 1. In Acts 17, "Paul boldly states that God has clearly witnessed to Himself *in* history but cannot be identified *with* anything in history or the world since He is Lord over both."[70]

---

[68] Boa and Bowman, 331.

[69] Boa and Bowman, 332.

[70] Greg L. Bahnsen, *Presuppositional Apologetics: Stated and Defended*, edited by Joel McDurmon (Powder Springs, GA; Nacogdoches, TX: American Vision; Covenant Media Press, 2008), 43.

In Romans 1, Paul describes how men, in their sinfulness, suppress their knowledge of God and practice idolatry (vv. 18-23). In Athens, Paul did not seek to find common ground with his hearers. Instead, he used their ignorance as his point of contact (Acts 17:23). He recognized that the Athenians were aware of God.

Because the truth about God is known but suppressed, presuppositionalism "appeals to what the sinner knows in his heart of hearts. It does not begin with or build upon what the sinner professes with darkened mind and vain reasoning."[71] Presuppositionalism can be especially useful in showing how the errors of non-Christian worldviews arise not merely from logical mistakes or factual inaccuracy but from religious rebellion.[72]

The Role of Scientific Apologetics

Defining Scientific Apologetics. "Scientific apologetics involves using scientific evidences to argue for the biblical God as the creator of the universe."[73]

---

[71] Bahnsen, 46.

[72] John M. Frame, "Presuppositional Apologetics," in *Five Views on Apologetics*, edited by Stanley N. Gundry and Steven B. Cowan, Zondervan Counterpoints Collection (Grand Rapids, MI: Zondervan, 2000), 223.

[73] Fernandes, 214.

Prominent scientific apologists in the Intelligent Design (ID) movement include Michael Behe, William Dembski, Philip Johnson, Hugh Ross, and Jonathan Wells. ID proponents offer scientific arguments against evolution. [74]

Science provides evidence of an Intelligent Designer of the universe. That evidence includes the fine-tuning of the universe and the specified complexity of the information found in biological life. One major piece of evidence used against evolution is the failure of the fossil record to reflect Charles Darwin's *tree of life*.[75] Darwin's tree is "the theory that all organisms are somehow related."[76]

Strengths of Scientific Apologetics. Scientific apologetics depends significantly on the work of ID proponents. A strength of the ID movement is that many scientists, be they old-earth, young-earth, Christian, or non-Christian, can unite under the ID banner. Without discounting the importance of controversial issues such as the age of the earth, science can help lead people to the Designer. Ross refers to another strength of scientific

---

[74] Fernandes, 214-16.

[75] Fernandes, 214-16.

[76] Kurt P. Wise, *Faith, Form, and Time: What the Bible Teaches and Science Confirms about Creation and the Age of the Universe* (Nashville, TN: Broadman & Holman, 2002), 111.

apologetics as he explains how a simple explanation of what the Bible teaches about creation can help resolve the objections of unbelievers. Some objections to Christianity are based more on the mind than the will.[77]

Weaknesses of Scientific Apologetics. A potential weakness of the ID movement from the perspective of scientific apologetics is that ID proponents do not necessarily claim to be religious. They sometimes express a commitment to going no further than the scientific evidence permits.[78] One of the movement's strengths (uniting many scientists under the same banner) could be a weakness if there is a lack of willingness to grapple with the theological implications of ID.

Another related weakness of ID is its lack of a historical narrative. ID advocates can agree there was a Designer, but they do not give the same answers to the *how*, the *when*, and the *by whom* questions. There is value in using science to point to the Designer, but the ultimate goal of the apologist should be to see people come to faith in the God of the Bible. Science can be a tool in that process, but there is a limit to how far science alone can take a person.

---

[77] Tim Stafford, "Church in Action: Hugh Ross's Apologetics Hot Line," *Christianity Today* (Carol Stream, IL: Christianity Today, 1991), volume 35, number 3, 21-22.

[78] Fernandes, 214.

Illustrating Scientific Apologetics. Ross founded the scientific apologetics ministry *Reasons to Believe* in 1986. According to research conducted at that time, "40 percent of Americans were essentially immune to traditional evangelism because of a mindset of scientific rationalism."[79] Even if that percentage has changed in the intervening years, it still demonstrates a cultural need for this apologetic methodology.

Ross offered the blunt assessment that "every scientist knows there is a God. He struggles with his pride."[80] Frank Britton points out that science "deepens your appreciation and love for the Lord. If he shows so much concern for the smallest detail of creation, he can certainly care for me."[81]

Given the esteem in which science is regarded by many people, scientific apologetics has a role in responding to the objections of scientifically-minded unbelievers. It can also draw believers closer to the God of creation.

---

[79] As cited in Stafford, 23.

[80] Stafford, 22.

[81] Stafford, 23.

The Role of Comparative Religious Apologetics (CRA)

Defining CRA. Walter Martin, an expert on non-Christian cults, was a practitioner of what Fernandes calls "comparative religious apologetics."[82] Martin defined a cult as "a group of people gathered about a specific person or person's misinterpretation of the Bible."[83] Despite their significant deviations from historic Christianity, members of these groups often claim to be Christian.

Comparative religious apologetics involves refuting non-Christian belief systems. Some specific groups Martin addressed in his writings include Mormonism, Jehovah's Witnesses, Christian Science, the Unity School of Christianity, the Unification Church, and the New Age Movement. Comparative religious apologists attempt to make the case for Christianity by refuting non-Christian worldviews.[84]

Strengths of CRA. A strength of comparative religious apologetics is that it meets a definite need. There are many non-Christian worldviews and ideas that apologists must challenge.[85]

---

[82] Fernandes, 235.

[83] Walter Martin, *The Kingdom of the Cults: The Definitive Work on the Subject* (Grand Rapids, MI: Bethany House, 2019), 13.

[84] Fernandes, 235-50.

[85] Fernandes, 250.

Another strength of this approach is that refuting non-Christian worldviews can be done logically. It is crucial to have a basic understanding of the laws of logic before engaging in worldview evaluation. Worldviews that violate a law of logic can be demonstrated to be irrational and, therefore, unworthy of belief.

Weaknesses of CRA. One weakness of comparative religious apologetics is that refuting non-Christian worldviews, while important, does not automatically establish the truthfulness of the Christian worldview. Demonstrating the superiority of theism over other worldviews does not prove Christianity is the most superior version of theism. There is a need to go beyond refutation by making a positive case for Christianity.

A second weakness is that this approach may prompt the apologist to have a disrespectful or condescending attitude due to the emphasis on refuting other worldviews. Care must be taken to gently and respectfully challenge those who hold different perspectives.

Illustrating CRA. The usefulness of comparative religious apologetics can be illustrated with the problem of evil. Every worldview must provide some explanation of evil. The Christian apologist could explain that evil actually points toward God because, without God, there could be no good because God provides the perfect standard of what is good. There cannot be objective evil without objective good. There can only be objective good if God exists.[86] Peter Kreeft wonders, "If there is no God, where did we get the standard of goodness by which we judge evil as evil?"[87] This example is a straightforward way for an apologist to demonstrate the superiority of Christianity over atheism.

Conclusion

Francis Schaeffer wrote, "I do not believe that there is any one system of apologetics that meets the need of all the people."[88] An apologetic approach should be "shaped on the basis of love for the person as a person."[89] The dialogical apologist seeks to be flexible, wise, and loving as they assess their audience's needs.

---

[86] Frank Turek, *Stealing from God: Why Atheists Need God to Make Their Case* (Colorado Springs, CO: NavPress, 2014), 11.

[87] As quoted in Lee Strobel, *The Case for Faith: A Journalist Investigates the Toughest Objections to Christianity* (Grand Rapids, MI: Zondervan, 2000), 34.

[88] As quoted in Doug Powell, *Holman QuickSource Guide to Christian Apologetics* (Nashville, TN: Holman Reference, 2006), 371.

[89] Francis Schaeffer, as quoted in Powell, 371.

Discussion Starters

1. To what extent have you studied Christian apologetics? Before reading this essay, were you familiar with these apologetic methodologies? Have you seen any examples of these methodologies in practice, even if you did not know the name of the method?

2. Do you find one of these apologetic methodologies to be particularly appealing? If so, why? Have you used any of them personally? If so, how would you assess their effectiveness?

3. Do you agree that apologetic encounters should always be crafted according to the needs and interests of the audience? Why or why not?

4. How has this overview of apologetic methods equipped you to share your faith more effectively? What would you like to remember the next time you share your faith?

Essay Three
The Use of Questions

Introduction

On February 4, 2021, Wayne[1] called Elnora Bible Institute. He wanted to ask someone a Bible question. Daniel (the author), an instructor at the school, was in his office that afternoon. The school secretary requested that Daniel handle the call. After Daniel picked up, Wayne explained that he had been doing some reading and wanted to ask a question about the Trinity. He eloquently set up his initial question. The presentation seemed rehearsed, and Daniel soon wondered if he was talking to a Jehovah's Witness (JW).

Wayne was initially polite, referring to Daniel as an "intelligent gentleman." However, little progress was made in the conversation, mainly because Wayne persisted in interrupting Daniel's attempts to reply.

The focus of the conversation shifted from the original question to a presentation of JW theology. Wayne eventually identified himself as a JW. He would repeatedly ask challenging questions, interrupt Daniel's replies, and

---

[1] His name has been changed for privacy reasons.

then accuse Daniel of not answering the questions. His politeness ceased. He became rude, exemplified by this statement after about thirty-five minutes: "I am not even sure why we are having this dopy conversation."

When Daniel said he was not being given many opportunities to reply, Wayne apologized. Still, shortly after, he resumed his interruptions. Near the end of the phone call, Wayne accused Daniel of being proud and deceived. He also suggested that Daniel had his "head stuck in the sand." The interaction ended with Wayne essentially stating that he was giving up on Daniel.

Throughout the conversation, Wayne employed a variety of techniques. He posed as a question-asker, although his main goal was actually to promote his own views. Initially, he was polite and flattering, but he became aggressive and rude when Daniel refused to accept his views. He tried to overwhelm Daniel with a barrage of ideas. He mockingly laughed at much of what Daniel said during the latter part of the conversation.

Wayne was attempting pre-evangelism as a JW, and his behavior offers some important lessons – particularly on how not to use questions. Questions are a valuable tool that Christian apologists can use in pre-evangelism to show respect to the other person and direct the course of a conversation.

The Importance of Apologetics and Pre-evangelism

The Importance of Apologetics. Because pre-evangelism is an aspect of the task of apologetics, the reader must understand what apologetics is and why it is necessary. Those concepts are explained on pages 4-8 of this book.

The Need for Pre-evangelism. Kenneth O. Gangel defines *pre-evangelism* this way: "Teaching and witnessing done to prepare people to be able to understand [the] meaning and message of the gospel of Christ."[2] Similarly, Alex McFarland understands pre-evangelism as removing obstacles that might hinder unbelievers from receiving the gospel.[3]

The question could be asked, "If pre-evangelism is biblical, then why is it not done in the Bible?" In response, it could be noted that Moses employed a form of pre-evangelism in Genesis 1, as he distinguished God's activity in creating the world from the mythical accounts of the world's creation that were promoted by the pagan religions of his day. Elijah's confrontation with the prophets of Baal, as recorded in 1 Kings 18, demonstrated the superiority of

---

[2] Kenneth O. Gangel, *Acts*, volume 5, Holman New Testament Commentary (Nashville, TN: Broadman & Holman, 1998), 479.

[3] Alex McFarland, *10 Answers for Atheists: How to Have an Intelligent Discussion about the Existence of God* (Bloomington, MN: Bethany House, 2012), 154.

the God of Israel. Further examples could be drawn from the ministry of Jesus and the apostles.[4]

Pre-evangelism certainly does not guarantee that a person will come to faith. Still, it is an appropriate method to employ when relating with those who do not trust in the God of the Bible.

David Geisler and Norman Geisler offer three reasons why pre-evangelism is necessary in today's world. First, there is a diminishing level of spiritual openness. Not everyone is prepared to receive the gospel on the spot. Because people are at different places in their spiritual understanding and interest, the evangelist must carefully consider how to lead someone one step closer to Jesus.[5]

Second, there is an increasing rejection of moral absolutes and an indifference toward truth. Those attitudes may need to be challenged in an apologetic encounter. Third, there is a growing intolerance toward anyone who believes in absolute truth.[6]

---

[4] Norman L. Geisler and Ronald M. Brooks, *When Skeptics Ask: A Handbook on Christian Evidences*, revised and updated (Grand Rapids, MI: Baker Books, 2013), 5.

[5] David Geisler and Norman Geisler, *Conversational Apologetics: Connecting with People to Share Jesus* (Eugene, OR: Harvest House Publishers, 2014), 19-25.

[6] Geisler and Geisler, 21-25.

The Role of Conversational Apologetics.
Conversational apologetics is a concept that is closely related to pre-evangelism. The idea behind this approach to presenting the Christian faith is apparent in the word *conversation*. Conversational apologetics recognizes the importance of interaction and relationships in making the case for the Christian faith.[7]

The traditional emphasis in apologetics has been to start by answering the questions skeptics raise about Christianity. Today, however, many people are not even interested in asking the questions that apologists have traditionally addressed. That declining interest necessitates another apologetic approach.[8]

Using Jesus' parable of the soils (Matthew 13:19-23), it could be emphasized that it is essential to "cultivate good soil" in the heart of an unbeliever. That could include helping them see the distortions in their worldview. A more direct "preaching" approach to evangelism is likely to be ineffective if the cultivating or "seed-planting" step is skipped or done too quickly.[9]

---

[7] David Geisler, "What is Conversational Apologetics?," in *The Comprehensive Guide to Apologetics*, edited by Joseph M. Holden (Eugene, OR: Harvest House, 2024), 65.

[8] David Geisler, 65.

[9] David Geisler, 66.

In 1 Corinthians 3:6-7, Paul mentions that, while human evangelists have a role to play in the "planting" and "watering" of the gospel in a person's heart, God ultimately brings about the growth. Dan Story writes that "apologetics is often used by the Holy Spirit to lay a foundation for future conversion [. . .] apologetics is planting and watering (pre-evangelism). This is a necessary first step on the road to salvation for many people."[10]

According to Raymond Prigodich, a more direct approach to apologetics often assumes that "every unbeliever is potentially ready to respond to the gospel upon first hearing [. . .] regardless of their background or lack of prior exposure to Christian truth."[11] He refers to pre-evangelism as being more indirect, as recognizing the importance of establishing a relationship with an unbeliever and demonstrating the personal credibility of the apologist.

It may take time for an unbeliever to recognize the truthfulness of Christianity, acknowledge their need for the gospel, and count the cost of following Jesus. Their decision may be superficial, premature, and ultimately inauthentic

---

[10] Dan Story, *Engaging the Closed Minded: Presenting Your Faith to the Confirmed Unbeliever* (Grand Rapids, MI: Kregel Publications, 1999), 26.

[11] Raymond Prigodich, "Pre-evangelism," in *Evangelical Dictionary of World Missions,* edited by A. Scott Moreau, Harold Netland, and Charles van Engen (Grand Rapids, MI: Baker Reference Library, 2000), 782.

unless they are given that time. A wise evangelist will recognize that there is no one-size-fits-all approach to sharing the faith and that respect must be shown to everyone.[12] If the reader is unfamiliar with dialogical apologetics, reviewing the discussion on pages 32-40 of this book would be helpful.

Questions as a Tactic in Pre-evangelism

Defining Rabbinic Evangelism. Randy Newman observes that some evangelistic strategies sound similar to the approach taken by used car salesmen. He argues that effective evangelism should more closely follow the strategy of the rabbi Jesus than that of the salesman. That includes a willingness to listen in addition to speaking. It also includes inviting people to faith in Jesus rather than demanding and pressuring them into making "a decision." About this method, which he calls *rabbinic evangelism*, Newman states, "Perhaps the most important component to this kind of evangelism is answering questions with questions rather than giving answers."[13]

This approach can help someone see both sides of an issue, which can help them reflect more deeply on their

---

12 Prigodich, 782-83.

13 Randy Newman, *Questioning Evangelism: Engaging People's Hearts the Way Jesus Did* (Grand Rapids, MI: Kregel Publications, 2004), 26.

beliefs. Helping people think well is a critical component of the evangelistic task. Paul took a rabbinic approach in his missionary journeys. In Acts 17:2-3, he reasoned with Jews in the synagogue. He explained to them that Jesus needed to die and be resurrected. Newman understands the verbs in this passage to suggest that Paul's synagogue sessions involved a certain amount of give-and-take; they were not one-sided. Rabbinic evangelism is about more than simply reasoning with people about Christianity logically and rationally. Reason alone is not sufficient to persuade a person to come to faith.[14]

Newman warns against treating the gospel as a sales pitch about receiving a gift or having a better life. The benefits of salvation are essential, but the good news will not be understood by those who do not understand the bad news of human sin and the judgment that sin deserves. "If we were to try and convince someone to 'buy' the gospel, we'd shy away from some difficult words that need to be said. Confronting a prospect with unpleasant truths doesn't work in sales, but it is essential in evangelism."[15] In short, dialogue is more effective than a sales pitch.

---

[14] Newman, 33-35.

[15] Newman, 35-36.

Defining the Columbo Tactic. Gregory Koukl introduces what he refers to as the *Columbo tactic* by asking his readers to imagine being in a difficult conversational situation.[16] For example, he presents a scenario where someone declares that there is no rational proof for God's existence. Koukl asserts that in those situations, a person only has about a ten-second window to respond before the opportunity to offer an effective response disappears. The Columbo tactic provides a way to respond quickly, graciously, and productively in challenging conversations. This tactic involves the use of clarifying questions.[17]

To return to the objection that there is no rational proof for God, Koukl suggests asking questions such as these:

- "What do you mean by 'God'?"
- "What is irrational about believing in God?"
- "What evidence would you acknowledge as confirming God's existence?"
- "What arguments for the existence of God have you considered?"

---

[16] Gregory Koukl, *Tactics, 10th Anniversary Edition: A Game Plan for Discussing Your Christian Convictions* (Grand Rapids, MI: Zondervan, 2019), 52.

[17] Koukl, 52-54.

- "What problems did you see with those arguments?"[18]

Those questions help the apologist to understand more about the God the other person is rejecting. This line of questioning also helps to reveal if the person has honestly thought about their assertions or if they are just making statements that are not the result of careful reflection. Responding with questions in difficult situations has several advantages. First, it provides the apologist an opportunity to allow the challenger to explain more fully what they think. This takes the pressure off the apologist. He can collect more information rather than letting himself be put on the spot. The better he understands the challenger's position, the less likely he is to jump to conclusions and misrepresent that position in his response.[19]

Increased understanding will also increase the effectiveness of the apologetic response. A request for clarification shows respect for the other person because it demonstrates a commitment not to distort their perspective. It could be a conversation-killer if the apologist is accused of twisting the challenger's words.[20]

---

[18] Koukl, 54.

[19] Koukl, 55.

[20] Koukl, 55.

A second benefit of the Columbo tactic is that it sets the stage for thoughtful and respectful dialogue. It is possible to be relaxed and cordial in a conversation while still asking pointed questions that gently challenge the other person's thinking. Third, carefully selected questions can advance the conversation. Some questions can be used to gather information or make a point. For example, certain questions may help someone recognize a problem with their viewpoint. Even timid people can use this flexible and adaptable approach to stay in the "driver's seat" of the conversation.[21]

Koukl summarizes this method by writing, "The key to the Columbo tactic is to go on the offensive in an inoffensive way with carefully selected questions that advance the conversation. Never make a statement, at least at first, when a question will do the job."[22]

Lessons from Proverbs. Four valuable lessons about questions can be drawn from the book of Proverbs. First, arguments should be avoided. In Proverbs 17:14, starting an argument is compared to breaching a dam. Because of the potentially destructive consequences, it is wise not to let a conversation become argumentative. It is

---

[21] Koukl, 52, 55-56.

[22] Koukl, 57.

fruitless to offend someone (Proverbs 18:19). Some people will likely be offended no matter what the apologist does. Still, an attempt should be made not to cause unnecessary offense. Winning an argument is not the same as winning an unbeliever to faith in Jesus.[23]

Second, an attempt should be made to recognize fools. There is a time to stop an unproductive conversation. Some conversations should never even be started. If someone is more committed to airing their opinions than discovering the truth, it is not wise to force the issue (Proverbs 14:7; 18:2; 23:9).[24]

The apparent contradiction in Proverbs · 26:4-5 should be addressed. Those verses read, "4) Do not answer a fool according to his folly lest you become like him – even you. 5) Answer a fool according to his folly, or else he will be wise in his own eyes" (LEB). In the wisdom literature of the Old Testament, which includes Proverbs, the term *fool* refers to a person who is set in opposition to God. It does not refer to a person's intelligence level.

Jason Lisle explains those verses as a two-step strategy for dealing with fools. Verse 4 is the first step. The folly that a fool brings to a conversation is his fallacious

---

[23] Newman, 42.

[24] Newman, 43-45.

presuppositions about God and the world. To not answer a fool according to his folly means not to accept the foolish presuppositions that a fool brings to the discussion.[25]

Accepting faulty presuppositions, even if only for the sake of argument, is no way to have a meaningful conversation because nothing solid can be built on an inadequate foundation. For example, if an atheist requests that the Bible be left out of a discussion about God's existence and the Christian agrees to do so, that is yielding to the folly of the atheist. There is no reason for the Christian to do that. A simple example of the foolishness of atheism is that does not have an adequate explanation for the possibility of knowledge. Lisle believes that only the Christian worldview explains why knowledge is possible.[26] An atheist might claim to know that he is an atheist, but his worldview does not explain his ability to know anything.

The problem with answering the fool according to his folly is that it reduces the believer to the fool's level. Verse 5 contains the second of the two steps and does not contradict that point. This verse instructs the believer to help the fool see his foolishness. For example, a relativist could declare, "There are no absolutes." The apologist

---

[25] Jason Lisle, *The Ultimate Proof of Creation: Resolving the Origins Debate* (Green Forest, AR: Master Books), 71-72.

[26] Lisle, 71-74.

should not accept that conclusion, but he should help the relativist recognize where that position leads. This could involve asking, "Is that an absolute statement? How can you make an absolute statement if absolute statements are not possible? How could any statement be true if there are no absolutes?" Relativism is self-refuting.[27]

Lisle refers to these verses as presenting the "Don't answer, answer" strategy. The two aspects of this strategy are to avoid accepting the fool's presuppositions and to show what would result if those presuppositions were true.[28] A system such as relativism leads only to contradictions.

Returning to the lessons about questions from Proverbs, a third point is to remember that all people have value in God's sight. That should shape how an apologist treats those with whom he has the opportunity to interact. This can include simple things such as appreciating them, smiling, remembering their names, listening to them respectfully, and showing a sincere interest in them. Proverbs 25:21-22 teaches that even enemies should be treated graciously.[29]

---

[27] Lisle, 74.

[28] Lisle, 71-75.

[29] Newman, 45-48.

Fourth, the power of the tongue must be remembered. The words of a righteous person "can bring forth wisdom (Proverbs 10:31), rescue the wicked (12:6), bring healing (12:18; 16:24; 15:4), commend knowledge (15:2), promote instruction (16:21, 23), and have the power of life and death (18:21)."[30] By contrast, "a lying tongue hates those it hurts" (26:28), is like a scorching fire (16:27), gushes folly (15:2), pierces like a sword (12:18), and lies in wait for blood (12:6)."[31] To speak without thinking is worse than being a fool (Proverbs 29:20). These verses do not call for complete silence. Instead, the tongue must be used wisely.[32]

The Importance of Educated Questions. Effective questions can be asked when something is known about the other person's beliefs. Studying different religions and worldviews can equip the apologist to ask specific questions. Such a study could also help the apologist know which issues should be given particular attention in the dialogue. A well-phrased question is a mirror to help someone see their worldview more accurately.[33]

---

[30] Newman, 48-49.

[31] Newman, 49.

[32] Newman, 49.

[33] David Geisler, 67-68.

Questions have tremendous power, as the former Mormon David Reed expressed: "A person can close his ears to facts he does not want to hear, but if a pointed question causes him to form the answer in his own mind, he cannot escape the conclusion – because it's a conclusion that he reached himself."[34]

To illustrate the importance of having some background knowledge, an apologist could ask a Muslim, "Since the Qur'an acknowledges that Jesus was sinless but Muhammad was a sinner, does it make sense to think that Muhammad was a greater prophet than Jesus? How could he be greater if he was a sinner?" That type of question could cause a Muslim to think more deeply about his beliefs.

Jesus' Use of Questions

Mark 10:17-22. Jesus was a master of answering questions with questions. As recorded in this passage, a young man approached Jesus and asked what he needed to do to be saved. Jesus asked why the man called him a good teacher, given that only God is good. He went on to remind the man of God's commandments. The man claimed that he obeyed those laws, which led Jesus to assert that one thing

---

[34] As quoted in David Geisler, 68.

was still lacking. This man needed to lay aside his earthly treasure and pursue heavenly treasure.

Some interpreters understand Jesus' reply to be an attempt to emphasize that he should not be identified with God. However, Jesus did not say, "I am not divine." His question seems designed to prompt the young man to think about the motive behind the original question. Jesus essentially asked the young man, "Do you realize that by calling me good you are associating me with God?" As R. Kent Hughes writes, "Jesus was attacking the man's shallow use of the word to get him to think about what he was saying, with the purpose of elevating him to understand that *Jesus really is God!*"[35]

As demonstrated by his response to this conversation, the young man was unprepared to grapple with the implications of Jesus' deity. This passage exemplifies how a question can help a person come to terms with what they genuinely believe.

Luke 8:43-48. Similarly, Jesus used a question in this passage that could elicit a statement of faith. As Jesus was navigating through a large crowd, a woman with a discharge of blood touched the fringe of his clothing. She was healed immediately. Although she had attempted not to

---

[35] R. Kent Hughes, *Mark: Jesus, Servant and Savior*, volume 2, Preaching the Word (Westchester, IL: Crossway Books, 1989), 62.

make herself obvious, Jesus wanted to engage with her. He asked who touched him. Even though the disciples pointed out to Jesus that he was surrounded by a crowd, he knew that healing power had gone out of him. The woman eventually fell before him and stated that she had been healed.

Jon Courson understands Jesus' question as intended to allow this woman to offer a public testimony about what had happened to her.[36] She was prompted to make a public statement of faith that she likely would not have made otherwise. This passage demonstrates the value of reaching out in conversation to even those who wish to be ignored.

Luke 9:18-20. Another example of using questions to draw out a public statement of faith is found in this passage. Jesus asked his disciples what the crowds thought about his identity. The answer he received was that the crowds regarded him as a prophet. He then made the question much more personal as he asked what the disciples thought about his identity. In response, Peter asserted that Jesus is the Christ. Jesus did not ask his questions out of pride. Rather, he asked his questions out of a recognition that a person's eternal destiny hinges on what they believe

---

[36] Jon Courson, *Jon Courson's Application Commentary* (Nashville, TN: Thomas Nelson, 2003), 346.

about him. As Warren Wiersbe writes, "It is impossible to be wrong about Jesus and right with God."[37]

A personal question like the one Jesus asked got right to the heart of an eternally weighty matter. As this passage exemplifies, there is a time to directly question someone about their beliefs.

John 5:1-9. The story recorded in this passage happened at the Pool of Bethesda in Jerusalem. In an encounter with a man who had been an invalid for thirty-eight years, Jesus asked if he wanted to be healed. The man declared that he had no one to help him get into the pool at the times when supposedly a person could be healed. Without using the pool, Jesus healed him. Why did Jesus use a question? It may seem unnecessary for Jesus to ask the man if he wanted to be healed. After all, the man was an invalid, so of course, he would wish to be healed.

Andreas Köstenberger says of Jesus' question, "Most likely, it is designed to elicit the man's perspective on the obstacle to his cure [. . .] The man's response makes clear that he could not see past the water as his healing agent."[38] After the man avoided giving a direct answer to Jesus and

---

[37] Warren W. Wiersbe, *The Bible Exposition Commentary*, volume 1 (Wheaton, IL: Victor Books, 1996), 206.

[38] Andreas J. Köstenberger, *John*, Baker Exegetical Commentary on the New Testament (Grand Rapids, MI: Baker Academic, 2004), 180.

instead stressed his faith in the pool, Jesus remarkably healed him by simply speaking. This passage highlights how a direct question can clarify the main issue even when an indirect answer is offered.

Examples of Questions and Scenarios

A Three-Tiered Framework. Paul Copan provides a helpful three-tiered framework for pre-evangelism. Those three tiers are Truth – God – Jesus. The first level is about establishing the foundation, which is the inescapability and undeniability of truth. Establishing such a foundation is vital if knowledge is to be considered possible.[39]

When in conversation with a relativist (someone who denies the existence of absolute truth), it could be helpful to ask these types of questions:

- "Why are you opposed to absolute truth?"
- "Would you be open to truth if it could be shown to you that it does exist?"
- "Do you realize that your position is self-refuting, namely, that you are claiming as a universal truth that there is no universal truth?"

The purpose of these questions is to challenge the relativist's thinking. Copan explains the importance of this

---

[39] Paul Copan, *"True for You but Not for Me"* (Minneapolis, MN: Bethany House, 2009), 16.

step by remarking, "Without belief in objective truth, the gospel message will fall on deaf ears."[40]

The focus of the second level is on considering the fundamental alternative worldviews. Several of the major worldviews are theism (belief in one God), atheism (lack of belief in God), and pantheism (the belief that all is God). Every worldview has its answers to the critical questions of life:

- "Why is there something rather than nothing?"
- "How did the universe originate?"
- "Where do people get their sense of morality?"

A belief in an intelligent, powerful, and personal Creator provides a solid foundation to answer those questions, especially compared to the deficiencies of alternative worldviews.[41]

If someone is willing to consider theism as a worldview, there could be a progression to the third level, evaluating which theistic worldview is the most plausible. The three options are Judaism, Islam, and Christianity. The task of apologetics includes presenting evidence for the reliability of the Bible and the resurrection of Jesus. Copan

---

[40] Copan, 16.

[41] Copan, 16-17.

argues that the evidence for Christianity points to it being more plausible than Judaism or Islam.[42]

Every worldview needs to answer these types of questions:

- "How do you explain the way Jesus fulfilled Old Testament prophecies?"
- "How do you make sense of the evidence for the resurrection of Jesus?"
- "How do you explain the uniqueness of Jesus?"

Questions to Use as Conversation Starters. Several sections of this essay present sample questions that could be used in different situations.[43] It is important to be gracious to the other person. A respectful way to start would be to ask, "Are you willing to have a conversation with me?" It is important not to force a discussion with someone who is unwilling to talk.

If the person is willing, these questions could help focus the discussion on spiritual matters:

- "What are you looking for in life? Have you found it?"
- "Do you have a religious background?"

---

[42] Copan, 17.

[43] Some of the questions presented in this section are adapted from an unpublished document that was used in a mission training program the author attended.

- "Do you believe there is a God? Why or why not?"

- "What do you think about Jesus? Have you ever considered the facts about Jesus?"

- "What is the most important thing in the world to you? When you die, what will be the most important thing to you?"

- "What do you think will happen to you after you die? Do you think you will go to heaven? Why or why not?"

- "How would you describe your spiritual journey?"

Questions to Use to Continue a Conversation. The questions in the previous section allow the apologist to learn more about the person with whom they are interacting. The apologist should be willing to be flexible and craft his responses as the conversation develops. As the other person shares his beliefs, these questions might be helpful:

- "What do you mean by that?"

- "How did you come to that conclusion?"

- "Where did you get your information?"

- "What if you are wrong?"

For example, if a person mentions that they believe in reincarnation, those questions could prompt them to think about what they believe and whether or not they have good reasons for their beliefs.

If the person mentions they practice a particular religion, such as Islam, the apologist could ask information-gathering questions such as these:

- "How did you become a Muslim?"
- "What does it mean to be a Muslim?"
- "What are the main beliefs of a Muslim?"

Questions to Use to Initiate a Gospel Presentation. People must recognize their sin to realize how the gospel provides a solution. Numerous questions could be used to set the stage for a presentation of the gospel:

- "Would you consider yourself to be a good person? If so, do you think your goodness can save you? If not, are you willing to consider something that addresses your lack of goodness?"
- "Do you think you have kept the Ten Commandments? If God would judge you by the Ten Commandments, would you be innocent or guilty?"

- "Will you go to heaven or hell? Does that concern you?"

- "Have you ever thought about how sin is an affront to an infinitely holy God who cannot tolerate sin?"

Questions to Use in Response to Two Common Objections. One common objection raised by non-Christians is expressed in the statement, "It does not matter what you believe as long as you are sincere." Various questions might be helpful to use in response to that idea:

- "What do you mean by *sincere*?"

- "Does this mean that a person cannot be sincerely wrong?"

- "Does this mean that, because I am sincere, you do not think I am wrong?"[44]

- "Why do you think a person's sincerity is more important than whether or not their belief is grounded in the truth?

- "Should a math teacher be expected to accept any answer to a question as long as the student is sincere?"

---

[44] Geisler and Geisler, 163-64.

Another common objection is, "It is arrogant to claim that Jesus is the only way to God." The apologist must help the critic think about that statement:

- "Is it always judgmental to think someone is wrong?"[45]

- "What do you mean by *arrogant*?"

- "Am I arrogant and immoral for believing what I sincerely think is true? What else can I do but believe it?[46]

- "Have you considered the evidence for the uniqueness of Jesus? Is it possible that there is good reason to believe that Jesus is the only way to be saved?"

- "Do you understand that I believe Jesus to be the only way to God because he is the only one who solved our sin problem?"

The Top Five Questions. Five simple questions can be used in the process of conversational apologetics. The first question is, "Really?" As an example, an apologist could respond to a statement about all religions being the same by asking, "Do you really think that all religions are

---

[45] Geisler and Geisler, 166-67.

[46] William Lane Craig, *On Guard: Defending Your Faith with Reason and Precision* (Colorado Springs, CO: David C Cook, 2010), 269-70.

basically the same?" The second question is, "What do you mean by that?" For example, it could be asked, "What do you mean when you say all religions are basically the same?" The third question is, "How did you come to that conclusion?" As an example, the apologist could ask, "How did you come to be persuaded that all religions are basically the same?"[47]

The fourth of the top five questions is "So?" Another version is "So what?" For example, "So? Hinduism and Buddhism have some similarities, but are there not also substantial differences?" Put another way, "Hinduism and Buddhism have similarities, but so what? Does that mean they are both right? What does this have to do with the evidence for Christianity?"[48]

The final question is, "Is it possible?" As an illustration, "Is it possible that only one religion is true and all the others are false? Since different religions have different views of God, is it not plausible to think that only one religion can be right?"[49] These types of questions are

---

[47] Randy Newman and Joel S. Woodruff, *Conversational Apologetics Course: Practicing the Art of Sharing Your Faith with Others* (Springfield, VA: C. S. Lewis Institute, 2014), 60.

[48] Newman and Woodruff, 60.

[49] Newman and Woodruff, 60.

helpful to get people to think, to expose contradictions, and to identify topics for discussion.[50]

Conclusion

Koukl states about his work as an apologist, "My aim is never to win someone to Christ. I have a more modest goal, one you might consider adopting as your own. *All I want to do is put a stone in someone's shoe.* I want to give that person something worth thinking about."[51]

Questions can be used effectively in the process of planting a stone in the shoe of an unbeliever by leading them to reflect on what they believe and why they believe what they do. While the use of questions is not the only approach to employ, it can be a valuable tool in the toolbox of a wise apologist. Jesus used questions effectively, and his evangelists would do well to consider how to incorporate question-asking into their apologetics ministries.

---

[50] Newman and Woodruff, 70-72.

[51] Koukl, 46.

Discussion Starters

1. Do you think that pre-evangelism is necessary? Why or why not? Were there obstacles that you needed to address before you came to faith? What barriers to faith have you heard expressed by other people?

2. What additional reasons can you think of for why apologetics is necessary? What else can we learn from the Bible about interacting with skeptics and seekers?

3. What do you think about Koukl's goal of putting a stone in someone's shoe? Do you think an apologist should seek to accomplish more than that in every apologetic encounter? If so, why?

4. Have you ever used questions in evangelistic conversations? If so, what have you learned? Can you think of someone you would like to converse with using this question-asking approach?

Essay Four

The Death and Resurrection of Jesus

Introduction

Is it historically factual that Jesus of Nazareth died on the cross and was raised to life three days later? Islam and Christianity part ways in response to that question. This disagreement highlights a critical distinction between the world's two largest religions. Islamic theology denies the Christian teaching about Jesus' death and resurrection. These events are foundational to the Christian doctrine of salvation and are "the central proof of Christ's claim to be the Son of God in human flesh."[1]

If a Christian apologist is to interact thoughtfully with Muslims, it is necessary to have accurate knowledge of the Islamic understanding of Jesus' death and resurrection. It is also essential to be familiar with the historical evidence for these events. The numerous alternative explanations for the death and resurrection of Jesus all fail to account for that evidence. Christianity accounts well for the historical evidence and is, therefore, shown to be superior to Islam.

---

[1] Norman L. Geisler and Abdul Saleeb, *Answering Islam: The Crescent in Light of the Cross*, second edition (Grand Rapids, MI: Baker Books, 2002), 234.

The Muslim View of Jesus' Death and Resurrection

Brief Comparison of the Christian and Muslim Views. On the surface, Islam and Christianity may seem to have similar beliefs about Jesus. Muslims and Christians both speak about Jesus' death and resurrection, as well as his virgin birth, ascension, and second coming.[2] However, care must be taken to avoid being led astray by the apparent similarities between these two religions.

The Bible teaches that Jesus experienced death by crucifixion at the hands of the Romans (Matthew 27:24-56; Mark 15:6-41; Luke 23:6-49; John 19:1-37). The Jewish religious leaders arranged for Jesus to go on trial before the Roman authorities. According to the Bible, the theological significance of Jesus' death is that his blood is a propitiation (Romans 3:25; 1 John 2:2). A propitiation is an offering that takes away wrath.[3]

Jesus' blood atones for sin. It is how God's wrath against human sin is satisfied, which allows for reconciliation between a holy God and sinful people (Colossians 1:19-22). In reconciliation, there is a restored relationship between two previously opposed parties.

---

[2] Geisler and Saleeb, 279.

[3] The Greek words behind this New Testament concept are defined in William Arndt, Frederick W. Danker, and Walter Bauer, *A Greek-English Lexicon of the New Testament and Other Early Christian Literature* (Chicago: University of Chicago Press, 2000), 473-74.

The biblical teaching about Jesus' death is incomplete without the affirmation of his resurrection from the dead three days later (Matthew 28:1-10; Mark 16:1-8; Luke 24:1-12; John 20:1-18). The resurrection event is theologically significant for numerous reasons, including how it confirms that Jesus is the Son of God (Romans 1:4).

Norman Geisler and Abdul Saleeb summarize the Muslim view of Jesus' death: "Most Muslims do not believe Jesus died on the cross, and none believe he paid the penalty for the sins of the world there."[4] Additionally, "while Islam teaches the resurrection of Jesus, it is usually only viewed as part of the general resurrection on the last day."[5] Muslims believe that Jesus ended his time on earth by ascending to heaven. Still, a resurrection from the dead is not thought to have preceded Jesus' ascension. If a Muslim scholar would affirm that Jesus was crucified, he would likely be deemed a heretic. The opposition to this is so strong that some Muslims consider even a belief in the crucifixion of Jesus to be demonic in origin.[6]

The Basis of the Islamic View. The vehement rejection by Muslims of Jesus' crucifixion is grounded in a

---

[4] Geisler and Saleeb, 279.

[5] Geisler and Saleeb, 279.

[6] Geisler and Saleeb, 279-80.

single verse from their primary religious text, the Qur'an.
This verse is Surah 4:157, which is quoted here along with
the following verse:

> 157. That they said (in boast), "We killed Christ
> Jesus the son of Mary, the Apostle of Allah"—but
> they killed him not, nor crucified him, but so it was
> made to appear to them, and those who differ
> therein are full of doubts, with no (certain)
> knowledge, but only conjecture to follow, for of a
> surety they killed him not—
> 158. Nay, Allah raised him up unto Himself; and
> Allah is Exalted in Power, Wise—[7]

Muslims use Surah 4:157 to support their claim that
Jesus' death by crucifixion only *appeared* to happen. In
Islamic theology, Jesus will be in heaven until the end
times. At that point, he will return to Earth, complete his
mission, and die. Muslims disagree about how to interpret
Surah 4:157, with some holding to the substitution theory
and others to the swoon theory.

The Substitution Theory. According to the
substitution theory, someone who had been made to
resemble Jesus was crucified.[8] This theory actually precedes

---

[7] Abdullah Yusuf Ali, translator, *The Meaning of the Holy Qur'an*
(Bellingham, WA: Logos Bible Software Research Edition, 2004), Surah
4:157-158.

[8] Daniel Janosik, *The Guide to Answering Islam: What Every
Christian Needs to Know about Islam and the Rise of Radical Islam* (Cambridge,
OH: Christian Publishing House, 2019), 289.

Islam, although it is now most commonly taught by Muslims. Forms of this theory emerged in the second century of Christian history as opponents of Christianity sought to discredit belief in Jesus' death and resurrection. The second-century teacher Basilides the Gnostic claimed that Jesus "changed form with Simon of Cyrene."[9]

Simon was crucified in Jesus' place. Jesus is said to have ridiculed his enemies for their error and then ascended to heaven. Other possible substitutes are the son of the widow of Nain (whom Jesus had raised from the dead) or the devil himself, whose plan to kill Jesus backfired.[10]

Most Muslims consider the substitute to have been either Simon of Cyrene or Judas Iscariot. It has also been suggested that the substitute was a human form rather than a human person.[11] Regardless of the identity of the substitute, the method God used to accomplish the substitution involved casting "a spell over the enemies of Jesus in order to rescue him."[12]

---

[9] Norman L. Geisler, *Baker Encyclopedia of Christian Apologetics*, Baker Reference Library (Grand Rapids, MI: Baker Books, 1999), 147.

[10] Geisler, *Baker Encyclopedia,* 147.

[11] Geisler, *Baker Encyclopedia,* 147-48.

[12] James Leo Garrett Jr., *Systematic Theology: Biblical, Historical, and Evangelical*, second edition, volume 2 (Eugene, OR: Wipf & Stock, 2014), 99.

The apocryphal *Gospel of Barnabas* teaches that Judas died in Jesus' place.[13] Although that account is appealed to by Muslims, it is a questionable document to use since it was written during the fourteenth or fifteenth century. Why should it be trusted to teach about Jesus reliably? Furthermore, the author was a Christian who converted to Islam, which explains its popularity amongst Muslims.[14]

Islamic arguments for the substitution theory often focus on alleged contradictions in the biblical record. It is argued that since the Gospel accounts disagree about Easter Sunday, the writers must have been confused and unsure about what really happened.[15] An example of a seeming contradiction is that Matthew refers to one angel as being at the tomb of Jesus (28:2), while Luke mentions two angels (24:4). Those discrepancies are thought to undermine the reliability of the biblical text.

The substitution theory includes a miracle, namely, Allah simply made it appear that it was Jesus who died.[16] It has been insightfully noted that "Such a theory reveals more concerning Islam's offense at the cross of Jesus than about

---

[13] Geisler, *Baker Encyclopedia,* 67-69.

[14] Garrett, footnote 100 (page 99).

[15] Nabeel Qureshi, *No God but One: Allah or Jesus?* (Grand Rapids, MI: Zondervan, 2016), 172.

[16] Qureshi, *No God But One,* 173.

the identity of the one crucified in Jerusalem between two thieves."[17]

The Swoon Theory. Another way some Muslims understand Surah 4:157 is with the swoon theory, which is the idea that Jesus was put on the cross but did not actually die. Instead, he *swooned* but later revived while in the tomb. Interestingly, a verse from the Qur'an seems to contradict Surah 4:157.[18] In Surah 19:33, the child Jesus is quoted as saying to his mother from his cradle, "So peace is on me the day I was born, the day that I die, and the day that I shall be raised up to life (again)"![19]

A few Muslims are willing to grant that Jesus did die by crucifixion, but they still deny his resurrection. Daniel Janosik has determined that "most Muslims today believe that someone else was crucified and Allah miraculously took Jesus up to heaven alive."[20]

Regarding Surah 4:157, the swoon theory emphasizes one aspect of the verse ("they killed him not, nor crucified him"). The substitution theory emphasizes another aspect ("but so it was made to appear to them").

---

[17] Garrett, 99.

[18] Janosik, 289-90.

[19] Ali, Surah 19:33.

[20] Janosik, 290.

Nabeel Qureshi distinguishes between the theistic swoon theory and the naturalistic swoon theory. In the naturalistic view, Jesus somehow survived his crucifixion without divine intervention. That does not explain how Jesus could have presented himself to his followers as the Lord of life. Even if he had survived, he would have been bloody, mangled, and in desperate need of medical attention. In the theistic swoon theory, a miracle allowed Jesus to survive the cross.[21]

The Islamic argument behind the theistic swoon theory is summarized by this question: "If God can perform the grand miracle of raising Jesus from the dead, why can he not perform a lesser miracle of preserving him from death in the first place?"[22] This theory emphasizes God's ability to save Jesus from death.

Proponents of this theory could appeal to numerous aspects of the crucifixion story, including that Pontius Pilate did not want to kill Jesus, which supposedly may have led him to conspire with the Roman centurion or Joseph of Arimathea to ensure that Jesus would not hang on the cross for the typical length of time.[23]

---

[21] Qureshi, *No God But One*, 170-71.

[22] Qureshi, *No God But One*, 171.

[23] Qureshi, *No God But One*, 171.

It is also argued, based on Jesus' prayer in Gethsemane, that he did not want to die, and so he implored God to save him. Hebrews 5:7 says that Jesus prayed to the one who could save him from death. Since his prayer was heard, it must have been answered, meaning that Allah miraculously saved Jesus from death on the cross.[24]

Muslim Objections to Jesus' Death. Hammuda Abdalati declared, "The Muslim cannot entertain the dramatic story of Jesus's death upon the cross just to do away with all human sins once and for all."[25]

From a Muslim perspective, any notion that atonement for man's sin can be accomplished through Jesus' cross is a travesty of justice. Muslim objections to the atonement take three primary forms: historical, metaphysical, and moral. The historical objection is the claim that Jesus did not experience death on the cross.[26] The two primary Muslim theories on this point have already been discussed.

---

[24] Qureshi, *No God But One*, 172.

[25] As quoted in Jeff Myers and David A. Noebel, *Understanding the Times: A Survey of Competing Worldviews* (Manitou Springs, CO: Summit Ministries, 2015), 61.

[26] Richard Shumack, *The Wisdom of Islam and the Foolishness of Christianity: A Christian Response to Nine Objections to Christianity by Muslim Philosophers* (Sydney, Australia: Island View Publishing, 2014), 131.

The metaphysical objection is the claim that the atonement is incoherent because it does not make sense to affirm that God could die. While making a seemingly reasonable point, this objection also reflects a failure to understand that Jesus has both a divine nature (that could not die) and a human nature (that could and did die).[27]

The moral objection is the claim that the atonement is senseless and unjust. It is argued that the atonement, which involves someone bearing the sin of another, "contravenes the sensible principle of justice that each person must be held responsible for the morality of their actions."[28] The death of Jesus is thought to compromise God's mercy. It is not understood how it could be merciful for God to kill his own Son. Muslims believe that God would be more merciful to forgive sin without requiring a blood sacrifice.[29]

An additional aspect of the moral objection is the Muslim belief that "the major prophets in history have always been victorious against their enemies."[30] It is believed that a sovereign God would not permit one of his prophets

---

[27] Shumack, 132-33.

[28] Shumack, 133.

[29] Shumack, 133-34.

[30] Geisler, *Baker Encyclopedia,* 142.

to experience a disgraceful death such as crucifixion. Since Allah is sovereign, he would certainly, in Islamic thinking, rescue his prophet from that type of experience. As one Muslim asks, "Is it consistent with God's mercy and wisdom to believe that Jesus was humiliated and murdered the way he is said to have been?"[31]

Summary of the Muslim View. It was mentioned earlier that Surah 19:33 appears to contradict Surah 4:157 in that Jesus is quoted as speaking about the day of his death. From a Muslim perspective, there is no contradiction between these verses. Many Muslims believe that Jesus did not die on the cross but was instead taken by Allah up to heaven. It is from there that he will return to earth. At that point, he will experience death. Qureshi explains that a nearly universal aspect of Islamic theology is how "the Quran is understood to teach that Jesus is currently in heaven, awaiting his return to earth, after which he will initiate the latter days and then die before the final day of resurrection."[32]

To conclude this section, the Muslim view of Jesus' death and resurrection could be summarized with these three points:

---

[31] Geisler, *Baker Encyclopedia,* 143.

[32] Nabeel Qureshi, *Answering Jihad: A Better Way Forward* (Grand Rapids, MI: Zondervan, 2016), 138-39.

1. All Muslims agree that Jesus did not die on the cross for our sins.

2. Almost all Muslims believe that Jesus did not die on the cross at all but that someone else was crucified in his place, such as Judas [. . .] or Simon who carried Jesus' cross.

3. Almost all Muslims hold that Jesus did not die at all before he ascended into heaven but that he will die after his second coming and will be raised later with others in the general resurrection of the last days.[33]

The Historical Evidence for Jesus' Death and Resurrection

The Historicity of the Events. Wilbur M. Smith observed that many people highly value historical certainty. This commitment to historical certainty gives Christianity "added confirmation" because "Jesus of Nazareth belongs to the realm of history."[34] That Jesus lived between 5-6 B.C. and 30-32 A.D. is as historically ironclad as any fact from the ancient world.[35]

In direct opposition to any notion of the swoon or substitution theories, Smith emphatically declares "that we know more about [. . .] the hours immediately before and

---

[33] Geisler and Saleeb, 281-82.

[34] Wilbur M. Smith, *Therefore Stand* (New Canaan, CT: Keats Publishing, 1981), 359.

[35] Smith, 359.

after the actual death of Jesus [. . .] than we know about the death of any other one man in all the ancient world."[36]

The historical evidence for Jesus' resurrection is necessarily connected to the evidence for his death. Lee Strobel summarizes the case for Jesus' death and resurrection with six alliterative words: *execution* (Jesus did actually die), *empty tomb* (Jesus' women followers did not find a body in his tomb), *eyewitnesses* (the disciples saw the risen Jesus), *early accounts* (of Jesus' resurrection), *extra-biblical reports* (Jesus' life, death, and resurrection are mentioned in secular writings), and the *emergence of the church* (the church began shortly after Jesus' death).[37] Each of those strands of evidence will be considered in more detail.

Execution. In making the case for Jesus' execution, it is necessary to understand the nature of crucifixion and the preceding torture. As was the common practice, Jesus was scourged before his crucifixion. The whip the Romans used for scourging had a short handle to which they attached straps that were up to two feet long. To the loose end of the straps, they tied such things as lead balls, metal, rocks, and pieces of bone and glass. Such sharp objects

---

[36] Smith, 360.

[37] Lee Strobel, *The Case for Christianity Answer Book* (Grand Rapids, MI: Zondervan, 2014), 121-24.

would break the skin of the victim and often pull it away from the body, which would expose bones and organs.[38]

This horrific form of torture was undoubtedly capable of bringing about the death of the victim. The loss of blood would send the victim into hypovolemic shock as the heart would attempt to compensate for the depletion of bodily fluid.[39]

For those who survived the ordeal of scourging, the experience of crucifixion was even more gruesome. Spikes of five to nine inches in length were used to nail the victim's wrists to the cross. As those spikes crushed the median nerve, extreme pain was produced. A spike would also be used to secure the ankles. When the cross was raised to its vertical position, the victim's shoulders were dislocated. To breathe, victims had to push themselves up using the ankle spike.[40]

Victims could linger long on the cross, with death eventually coming through asphyxiation or heart failure. The executioner could break the legs of the victim to hasten death. Jesus' legs were not broken, but a Roman soldier did thrust a spear into his side. To those who suggest that Jesus

---

[38] Doug Powell, *Holman QuickSource Guide to Christian Apologetics* (Nashville, TN: Holman Reference, 2006), 270.

[39] Powell, 271.

[40] Powell, 271-72.

could have survived that process, Mark Powell demurs, writing that "There was no question whatsoever in the mind of the professional executioner that Jesus was dead."[41] This explanation of crucifixion renders the swoon theory implausible.

The substitution theory is also questionable for several reasons. First, it makes God a deceiver who caused people to think that it was Jesus who died. Admittedly, this is a theological rather than historical point, yet historical reasons can be offered. Second, the Qur'an does not provide an eyewitness account of Jesus' death. Third, the Qur'an contradicts the eyewitness historical record of the New Testament Gospels. Fourth, the substitution theory makes Jesus a false prophet because he predicted his death (Mark 9:31). That should be an unacceptable option for Muslims, who regard Jesus as God's prophet.

Strobel emphasizes that Christians "can rest assured that it really was Jesus on the cross, suffering for our sins just as he predicted, paying for our salvation just as he promised."[42]

Empty Tomb. William Lane Craig offers five lines of evidence to support the fact that a group of Jesus' women

---

[41] Powell, 272.

[42] Strobel, 120.

followers discovered his empty tomb on the Sunday following the crucifixion. First, the story of Jesus' burial is historically reliable. This supports the empty tomb story because it confirms that both Jesus' friends and enemies would have known the location of the tomb. Jesus' disciples would not have believed in his resurrection if his tomb had remained occupied.[43]

Additionally, if the tomb was not empty, Jesus' enemies would have been able to point to an occupied tomb, which would have been a death blow to the early Christian movement. The burial story is recorded in early, independent sources, including the creed in 1 Corinthians 15:3-8. Joseph of Arimathea is a surprising member of the burial story, and it is implausible that his presence in the story is a Christian invention because he was a member of the Jewish council that condemned Jesus.[44] A.T. Robinson declared Jesus' burial to be "one of the earliest and best-attested facts about Jesus."[45]

The second line of evidence is the early sources that independently report the discovery of Jesus' empty tomb. As has been mentioned, 1 Corinthians 15:3-8 is an early source.

---

[43] William Lane Craig, *On Guard: Defending Your Faith with Reason and Precision* (Colorado Springs, CO: David C Cook, 2010), 219-21.

[44] Craig, 221-24.

[45] As quoted in Craig, 224.

In this passage, the phrases "he was buried" and "he was raised" imply that his tomb was empty. Third, the empty tomb narratives in the Gospels offer powerful confirmation of the resurrection because of their simplicity and lack of legendary development. The Gospels simply do not possess the characteristics of a legend.[46]

Fourth, the women's discovery of the empty tomb is significant because women were not considered credible witnesses in first-century Jewish society. It is unlikely the early Christians would have invented such a detail. Finally, there is the initial Jewish response to Christian preaching. Matthew 28:11-15 records the Jewish leaders telling the soldiers to spread the word that the disciples stole the body of Jesus. Their desperate attempt to explain away the evidence presupposes that the tomb was empty.[47]

Eyewitnesses. The testimony of eyewitnesses is a crucial form of evidence in legal proceedings. Dan Story states, "The most compelling and irrefutable evidence for the resurrection of Jesus Christ comes from recorded eyewitnesses (legal testimony)."[48] Both Jesus' death and his

---

[46] Craig, 225-27.

[47] Craig, 228-29.

[48] Dan Story, *Christianity on the Offense: Responding to the Beliefs and Assumptions of Spiritual Seekers* (Grand Rapids, MI: Kregel Publications, 1998), 82.

post-resurrection appearances "are recorded either by eyewitnesses to the events or by the companions of eyewitnesses."[49] The Gospel accounts are primary source material. Peter and John took seriously their roles as eyewitnesses (2 Peter 1:16; 1 John 1:1-3).

The apostles would have been motivated to think about the truthfulness of the Christian message, for which they were willing to die. They would have had no reason to fabricate the Christian story. They had nothing to gain by concocting a story that would lead to their persecution. If the evidence for Jesus' death and resurrection were evaluated in a fair legal trial, the historicity of those events would be established beyond a reasonable doubt.[50]

Early Accounts. There are several indicators that 1 Corinthians 15:3-8 is an early Christian creed, such as Paul's use of the words "delivered" and "received." His use of these technical terms suggests he was passing on a tradition he had received from another source. Other indicators are the words or phrases in the creed that scholars regard as non-Pauline (such as "the Twelve") and the creed's stylized, parallel structure. The passage's structure points to an oral

---

[49] Story, 83.

[50] Story, 83.

and confessional origin. Scholars frequently date the text's origin to the middle of the 30s.[51]

It has been noted that 1 Corinthians 15 "preserves uniquely early and verifiable testimony. It meets every reasonable demand of historical reliability."[52] The apostles' sermons recorded in Acts are crucial early records. Luke 24:34 briefly mentions the appearance of the resurrected Jesus to Peter. This account is thought by some to be of greater antiquity than the reference to Peter in 1 Corinthians 15:5. Furthermore, Romans 1:3-4, Romans 10:9-10, and 2 Timothy 2:8 are three additional ancient creeds that testify to Jesus' resurrection.[53]

Extra-Biblical Reports. Numerous references to Jesus' death and resurrection exist in non-Christian sources, including Roman writings and Jewish rabbinic writings. Two Roman writers will be cited here. Around 73 A.D., Mara bar Serapion mentioned that the Jews experienced "the death of their wise king."[54] In approximately 110 A.D.,

---

[51] Gary R. Habermas, *The Historical Jesus: Ancient Evidence for the Life of Christ* (Joplin, MO: College Press Publishing Company, 1996), 152-54.

[52] Habermas, 156.

[53] Habermas, 149-50.

[54] C. A. Evans, "Jesus in Non-Christian Sources," in *Dictionary of Jesus and the Gospels*, edited by Joel B. Green and Scot McKnight (Downers Grove, IL: InterVarsity Press, 1992), 365.

Tacitus wrote that Pontius Pilate was the governor who sentenced "Christus" to death during the reign of Tiberius Caesar.[55]

There are several references in the rabbinic writings to the fact that Jesus of Nazareth was hung on the eve of Passover. Since crucifixion involved being hung on a cross, this can easily be understood as referring to crucifixion. In rabbinic writings, Jesus' resurrection is referred to in the context of him being a magician. The resurrection is said to have happened by "incantation."[56] It is also declared, "Woe to him who makes himself alive by the name of God."[57] While these non-Christian references do not prove the historicity of the events, they do provide substantial corroborating evidence.

Emergence of the Church. A final piece of historical evidence for Jesus' death and resurrection is the establishment of the Christian church in the first third of the first century A.D. Apart from Jesus' resurrection, there is no compelling explanation for why the church emerged on the scene of history when and where it did. In the words of the historian Philip Schaff, "The miracle of the

---

[55] Evans, 365.

[56] Evans, 367.

[57] Evans, 367.

resurrection and the existence of Christianity are so closely connected that they must stand or fall together."[58]

The church would not have emerged apart from the belief of Christians in the crucified and resurrected Jesus. The New Testament scholar C. F. D. Moule asked, "If the coming into existence of the Nazarenes [. . .] rips a great hole in history, a hole the size and shape of Resurrection, what does the secular historian propose to stop it up with?"[59] Critics are committed to denying Jesus' death and resurrection, and they are certainly free to do so. However, they also bear a burden of proof. They must offer a satisfactory counter-explanation for all of this evidence.

The Failure of Alternative Explanations

The Wrong Tomb Theory. The deficiencies of the substitution theory and the swoon theory have already been addressed. Two additional inadequate explanations will be refuted in this section. The wrong tomb theory grants that Jesus died, but it maintains that on the following Sunday

---

[58] As quoted in Barry R. Leventhal, "Why I Believe Jesus Is the Promised Messiah," in *Why I Am a Christian: Leading Thinkers Explain Why They Believe* (Grand Rapids, MI: Baker Books, 2001), 218.

[59] As quoted in Leventhal, 218.

morning, Jesus' followers went to the wrong tomb. They then mistakenly concluded that Jesus had been resurrected.[60]

This theory explains the empty tomb, at least to some extent. However, it does not explain the appearances of the resurrected Jesus, for which there is eyewitness testimony. It does not explain the conversion of Saul, who saw the risen Jesus. He did not come to faith simply because there was an empty tomb which supposedly had belonged to Jesus. The same could be said of James, who was previously skeptical about his half-brother's identity (e.g., Mark 3:21).[61]

There is no indication that anyone in the first century ever thought the wrong tomb was visited. The Jewish leaders would have undoubtedly corrected such an error. The solidly confirmed burial story indicates that the location of Jesus' tomb was well-known.[62]

The Hallucination Theory. It can be challenging to establish what exactly constitutes a hallucination, but one proposed definition is that it is "a conscious sensory experience that occurs in the absence of corresponding external stimulation [. . .] and has a sufficient sense of reality

[60] Josh McDowell and Sean McDowell, *Evidence That Demands a Verdict: Life-Changing Truth for a Skeptical World* (Nashville, TN: Thomas Nelson, 2017), 292.

[61] McDowell and McDowell, 292.

[62] McDowell and McDowell, 292-93.

to resemble a veridical perception."[63] A hallucinating person imagines something to be real when it is not. In such an encounter, "the subject does not feel he or she has direct and voluntary control over the experience."[64]

Advocates of this theory maintain that the disciples hallucinated visions (which were possibly guilt-induced) of the resurrected Jesus. A massive problem with this theory is that there is no reason to accept the possibility of group hallucinations. Hallucinations seem to be necessarily individual and subjective. This theory cannot adequately explain the appearances of Jesus.[65]

Not only did Jesus appear to groups, but the diversity of his appearances is challenged by the fact that hallucinations are generally one-time occurrences. In his resurrection appearances, Jesus was obviously physical, as he, for example, ate with and was touched by his disciples. This is not consistent with what takes place in a vision. Perhaps most importantly, the hallucination theory does not explain the empty tomb or the inability of the religious leaders to produce the corpse of Jesus.[66]

---

[63] McDowell and McDowell, 287.

[64] McDowell and McDowell, 287.

[65] McDowell and McDowell, 287-90.

[66] McDowell and McDowell, 290-92.

The Theological Importance of Jesus' Death and Resurrection

The Importance of Jesus' Death. The significance of these events to Christian theology can scarcely be overstated. The Christian apologist must have an accurate understanding of the implications of this event. It has been written that the crucifixion "is among the most historically certain and theologically pregnant events of Jesus' life."[67] The importance of Jesus's death is emphasized in the statement that "the Gospels see in this fact the accomplishment of the plan of God for the redemption of his people and the world."[68] It is "the means by which God has provided for salvation."[69]

The apostles' preaching in Acts emphasizes how the death of Jesus was the purpose of God (2:23). Jesus fulfilled his God-appointed role as the suffering servant through his death, as prophesied in Isaiah 53. Jesus predicted his death throughout the Gospels (e.g., Luke 9:22). After his

---

[67] J. B. Green, "Death of Jesus," in *Dictionary of Jesus and the Gospels,* edited by Scot McKnight (Downers Grove, IL: InterVarsity Press, 1992), 147.

[68] J. Dennis, "Death of Jesus," in *Dictionary of Jesus and the Gospels, Second Edition,* edited by Joel B. Green, Jeannine K. Brown, and Nicholas Perrin (Downers Grove, IL; Nottingham, England: IVP Academic, 2013), 172.

[69] J.B. Green, "Death of Christ," in *Dictionary of Paul and His Letters,* edited by Gerald F. Hawthorne, Ralph P. Martin, and Daniel G. Reid (Downers Grove, IL: InterVarsity Press, 1993), 201.

resurrection, Jesus told the disciples on the road to Emmaus that the Messiah needed to suffer (Luke 24:25-27). During his trial before Pontius Pilate, Jesus affirmed that the Roman governor was acting according to God's will (John 19:11).[70]

The New Testament presents the forgiveness of sins as a significant purpose of Jesus' death. In John 10:11, Jesus refers to himself as the *good shepherd*. Part of his work is sacrificing his life for his sheep (John 10:15), which expresses the love of both the Father and the Son (1 John 3:16; 4:10).[71]

In his role as sin-bearer, Jesus gave himself as a ransom (Mark 10:45; Hebrews 9:28; 1 Peter 2:24). Galatians 3:10-13 emphasizes Jesus' role as a redeemer from the curse of the law. Isaiah 53:5-6 predicts that the Messiah would be pierced and crushed for transgressions. Forgiveness of sins through the blood of Jesus allows humankind to be reconciled to God (Romans 5:11).[72]

The book of Hebrews teaches that Jesus is the fulfillment of the Old Testament sacrificial system. God's

---

[70] Francis Foulkes, "Death of Christ," in *Evangelical Dictionary of Biblical Theology*, edited by Walter A. Elwell, Baker Reference Library (Grand Rapids MI: Baker Book House, 1996), 157-58.

[71] Foulkes, 158.

[72] Foulkes, 158-59.

justice was satisfied through the death of the sinless Son of God (Romans 3:24-26). To summarize, Jesus' death is the way of salvation from God and also the path to acceptance by God.[73]

The Importance of Jesus' Resurrection. The resurrection of Jesus, which obviously would not have been possible apart from his death, has been referred to as "a kingpin of the Christian faith."[74] Christianity would be worthless if these events had not happened. 1 Corinthians 15:14 says, "But if Christ has not been raised, then our preaching is in vain, and your faith is in vain" (LEB).

Jesus' resurrection is a vital aspect of God's work of redemption. In Philippians 3:10, Paul refers to the redemptive work accomplished "by the power of his resurrection" (LEB). The New Testament presents Jesus' resurrection as a literal, historical, bodily resurrection. It is a requirement for salvation that a person believes that God raised Jesus from the dead (Romans 10:9).[75]

There are numerous theological implications of Jesus' resurrection for the Christian understanding of salvation.

---

[73] Foulkes, 159.

[74] Norman L. Geisler, *The Battle for the Resurrection* (Eugene, OR: Wipf & Stock Publishers, 1992), 107.

[75] Jack Cottrell, *The Faith Once for All: Bible Doctrine for Today* (Joplin, MO: College Press Publishing Company, 2002), 272.

First, the resurrection confirms Jesus' claims and, consequently, it demonstrates his deity. Jesus made many claims about himself, including that he is one with the Father (John 10:30), was sent from God (John 8:42), and has the authority to forgive sins (Matthew 9:2-8). From the perspective of Christian apologetics, the resurrection provides divine confirmation of Jesus' identity. It is a verifiable historical event confirming a faith that is rooted in Jesus' person and work.[76]

Second, the resurrection was devastating to Jesus' enemies. It was how Jesus destroyed the power of Satan, sin, and death (1 Corinthians 15:55-57; Colossians 2:15; Hebrews 2:14; 1 John 3:8). Third, it was through the resurrection that Jesus inaugurated his kingdom and his lordship over all things. The resurrected Jesus declared that all authority had been given to him (Matthew 28:18). Fourth, the resurrection validated the cross by making it unquestionably obvious that Jesus defeated his enemies (Colossians 2:12-15). The resurrected Jesus is at the right hand of God, where he intercedes for believers (Romans 8:34).[77]

Fifth, Jesus' resurrection originates the new creation. Jesus is the "firstborn from the dead" (Colossians

---

[76] Cottrell, 273-74.

[77] Cottrell, 274-77.

1:18). Jesus' resurrection begins God's work of new creation. Sixth, Jesus' resurrection reanimates the dead. Jesus' resurrected body is a prototype of how the dead bodies and spirits of humankind can be raised (1 Corinthians 15:49). Salvation is both physical (Romans 8:23) and spiritual (John 3:5). The final point is that the resurrection of Jesus renovates the universe. Believers should live in anticipation of the creation of the new heavens and new earth (2 Peter 3:13; Revelation 21:1-4). The entire created world needs redemption.[78]

Conclusion

James White articulates several key points when he asserts, "The Christian must recognize that, for the Muslim, the cross of Christ is a scandal."[79] Nevertheless, "Muslims must see that accepting the teaching of Surah 4:157 leaves them standing in direct opposition to the whole of history."[80] The teaching of this verse from the Qur'an "is [an] utterly insufficient basis for overthrowing the mountain of testimony to the crucifixion of Jesus on a hill outside

---

[78] Cottrell, 277-82.

[79] James R. White, *What Every Christian Needs to Know about the Qur'an* (Minneapolis, MN: Bethany House Publishers, 2013), 284.

[80] White, 284.

Jerusalem."[81] Is it historically factual that Jesus of Nazareth died on the cross and was raised to life three days later? The negative responses to this question all possess significant deficiencies. Christianity's affirmative response accounts for the historical evidence, thereby demonstrating that Christianity is superior to Islam.

Discussion Starters

1. What surprised you about the Muslim understanding of Jesus' death and resurrection?

---

[81] White, 285.

2. Have you ever encountered a view that denies Jesus' resurrection? If so, were you able to offer a meaningful response? How would you respond now?

3. Can you think of any other objections to Jesus' resurrection? How would you respond to those?

4. How would Christianity be different if Jesus' death and resurrection had not happened?

Essay Five
The Personhood of the Unborn Child

Introduction

The viewpoint known as moral relativism treats ethical decisions as nothing more than expressions of personal preference. Francis Beckwith and Gregory Koukl write about a consequence of moral relativism: "When morality is reduced to personal tastes, people exchange the moral question, What *is* good? for the pleasure question, What *feels* good?"[1] This shift in thinking produces a morality based on self-interest. That can impact a person's behavior in many ways, including in their treatment of other humans.

Beckwith and Koukl recount the following story. Jennifer was a nurse at the Los Angeles hospital where this happened. She tells the story from her perspective:

> One night a nurse on my shift came up to me and said, "Jennifer, you need to see the Garcia baby."
> There was something suspicious about the way she said it, though. *I see babies born every hour*, I thought.

---

[1] Francis J. Beckwith and Gregory Koukl, *Relativism: Feet Firmly Planted in Mid-Air* (Grand Rapids, MI: Baker Books, 1998), 20-21.

She led me to a utility room [. . .] There, lying on the metal, was the naked body of a newborn baby. "What is this baby doing here on this counter?" I asked timidly.

"That's a preemie born at nineteen weeks," she said. "We don't do anything to save them unless they're twenty weeks."

I noticed that his chest was fluttering rapidly. I picked him up for a closer look. "This baby is still alive!" I exclaimed. I thought they hadn't noticed.

Then I learned the horrible truth. The nurses knew, and it didn't matter. They had presented the baby to its mother as a dead, premature child.

Then they took him away and tossed him on the cold, steel counter in the lunch room until he died. His skin was blotchy white, and his mouth was gaping open as he tried to breathe.

I did the one thing I could think of. I held him in his last moments so he'd at least have some warmth and love when he died.

Just then one of the nurses – a large, harsh woman – burst into the room. "Jennifer, what are you doing with that baby?" she yelled.

"He's still alive…"

"He's still alive because you're holding him," she said. Grabbing him by the back with one hand, she snatched him from me, opened one of the stainless steel cabinets, and pulled out a specimen container with formaldehyde in it.

She tossed the baby in and snapped the lid on. It was over in an instant.

To them, this child wasn't human. In seven more days he would have qualified, but at nineteen weeks he was just trash.[2]

---

[2] Beckwith and Koukl, 21-22.

The authors conclude from this sobering story: "When persons are viewed as things, they begin to be treated as things."[3]

The *National Right to Life Committee*, a prominent anti-abortion organization, has calculated that 63,459,781 recorded abortions were performed in the United States between 1973 and 2019.[4] That was an average of over 3,500 abortions per day. In light of that statistic, Koukl asserts, "The most dangerous place for a baby to be in the land of the free and the home of the brave is resting in her mother's womb."[5]

What is an unborn child? Some pro-abortion proponents attempt to distinguish between humanness and personhood. Is such a distinction appropriate? What is a human? What makes someone a person? When does the unborn child acquire humanness and personhood? Those questions, which have significant ethical ramifications, will be explored in this essay.

---

[3] Beckwith and Koukl, 22.

[4] Cited by Gregory Koukl, *Street Smarts: Using Questions to Answer Christianity's Toughest Challenges* (Grand Rapids, MI: Zondervan Reflective, 2023), 225.

[5] Koukl, 226.

Abortion-Rights Arguments

When thinking about whether or not an unborn child possesses personhood, the options are either that a child is a person at the moment of conception or that a child becomes a person at some later point.

Abortion-rights advocates recognize, as their pro-life counterparts do also, that the critical question in the abortion debate is whether or not the unborn child is fully human. They realize that if the answer to this question is yes, then abortion is murder in nearly every situation, perhaps only excluding instances when the pregnancy endangers the life of the mother. These abortion-rights promoters recognize that the unborn entity is human in that it technically belongs to the species known as *homo sapiens*. Nevertheless, they do not regard the unborn entity as a person.[6] Four abortion-rights arguments will be summarized and evaluated.

The Argument from Decisive Moments. The essence of this argument is that there is some *decisive moment* in the child's development in which they become a person and acquire all the accompanying rights.

_____

[6] Francis J. Beckwith, *Politically Correct Death: Answering Arguments for Abortion Rights* (Grand Rapids, MI: Baker Books, 1993), 91.

The philosopher Michael Tooley dislikes the fact that *person* and *human being* are often used as synonymous terms. Tooley recognizes that persons have rights, but he attempts to distinguish between humanness and personhood. He does not consider every human being to be a person. According to James Eckman, this is Tooley's general rule: "An organism has a serious right to life only if it possesses the concept of a self as a continuing subject of experiences and other mental states and believes itself to be a continuing entity."[7]

Proponents of this view are likely to grant that individual human life begins at conception. However, they think that the unborn child is not worthy of protection until some later point. Tooley allows for infanticide at any point up to even a week after birth.[8]

The decisive moment view can take numerous forms. To list some of the possibilities, someone might place the decisive moment when personhood is achieved at the time the conceptus is implanted in the mother's womb, at the time when the child gains the *appearance of humanness*,

---

[7] James P. Eckman, *Biblical Ethics: Choosing Right in a World Gone Wrong*, Biblical Essentials Series (Wheaton, IL: Crossway Books, 2004), 36.

[8] Eckman, 36.

at viability, at the beginning of brain functioning, or at the child's birth.[9]

The Argument from Gradualism. In this view, "the unborn gradually gains more rights as it develops."[10] Stated another way, because an adult is more developed than a fetus, it has more rights than a fetus. A fetus, in turn, has more rights than a zygote. There is an increase in moral rights as someone progresses through the physical process of human development.[11]

As Amanda Roth explains it, "The development of moral status is a gradual process that occurs continuously throughout gestation. That means that later fetuses have more status than earlier ones; later abortions too are more grave morally."[12] She bluntly states that "while a 6- or 8-week embryo might have very minimal status, a fetus at 32 or 35 weeks has virtually identical moral status to a

---

[9] Beckwith, 95-105.

[10] Beckwith, 91.

[11] Beckwith, 91-92.

[12] Amanda Roth, "When does the fetus acquire a moral status of a human being? The philosophy of 'gradualism' can provide answers," The Conversation, June 30, 2022, https://the conversation.com/when-does-the-fetus-acquire-a-moral-status-of-a-human-being-the-philosophy-of-gradualism-can-provide-answers-185938 (accessed April 24, 2024).

newborn."[13] That is why "the earliest abortion is generally morally unconcerning to someone with a gradualist view, while third-trimester abortion is seen as a grave action that requires the strongest of moral reasons."[14]

Roth maintains that moral justification is required to end the life of a mid-pregnancy fetus who, at that stage of development, is in what could be called a *morally in-between position*.[15] She argues that "gradualism has the benefit of making sense of the public's strong support for early abortion, but hesitating about terminations in the second and third trimesters."[16]

The Argument from Performance and the Utilitarian Argument. The secular worldview does not make a connection between the fetus being a living human and possessing intrinsic value. This worldview, which denies the existence of both God and transcendent truth, contends that a human should not be "valued as a person

---

[13] Roth, "When does the fetus acquire a moral status of a human being?"

[14] Roth, "When does the fetus acquire a moral status of a human being?"

[15] Roth, "When does the fetus acquire a moral status of a human being?"

[16] Roth, "When does the fetus acquire a moral status of a human being?"

unless he or she operates at full human capacity or shows value to society."[17] That notion is found in both the argument from performance and the utilitarian argument.[18] Because these two abortion-rights arguments have some similarities, they will be introduced alongside each other.

The argument from performance assigns value to humans according to their ability to meet a set of conditions. It excludes individuals based on their failure to meet certain expectations. Those who do not meet the qualifications are not worthy of dignity or respect. While the criteria can vary, the possibilities include "self-awareness, rationality, sentience, desirability, ethnicity, economic productivity, gender, nationality, native language, beauty, age, health, religion, race, ethnicity, fertility, birth, and national origin."[19] Presumably, if a human could gain the desired condition(s), they would then be valued as a person. If they eventually lose their qualifications, they would lose their personhood as well.

The philosopher Peter Singer is a proponent of the utilitarian argument, which he defines this way: "The

---

[17] Jeff Myers, *Understanding the Culture: A Survey of Social Engagement* (Colorado Springs, CO: David C Cook, 2017), 207.

[18] Myers, 207.

[19] Myers, 207.

essence of the principle of equal consideration of interests is that we give equal weight in our moral deliberations to the like interests of all those affected by our actions."[20] Jeff Myers interprets what this means: "If those around us stand to lose more than we stand to gain by our existence, then it's better for us not to exist."[21]

Singer was willing to take his view to its logical conclusion. He promoted infanticide (killing a child up to a year after birth), especially of severely handicapped infants. He admitted that his view allows for even healthy infants to be killed. What matters most to Singer is not whether the child has a right to life but whether the parents would have an emotionally adverse reaction to killing their child. If the parents would not be adversely affected, then the killing can happen.[22]

This position implies that humans are simply a higher order of animals. The cognitive ability of humans may make them the highest order of animals, but, in this view, humans are still nothing more than that. Singer asserted in his famous book *Unsanctifying Human Life*, "The doctrine of the sanctity of human life, as it is normally

---

[20] As quoted in Myers, 207.

[21] Myers, 207.

[22] Myers, 207-08.

understood, has at its core a discrimination of species and nothing else."[23]

Singer's separation of biological humanness (which he considered a material trait) and personhood (which he considered a metaphysical trait) allows him to make that claim. Making personhood dependent on acquiring specific cognitive abilities means that, as Mary Jo Sharp writes, "Human value and worth are then based on the current status of these abilities, without which a human would cease to be a person."[24] The implication of this is that when the intrinsic value of humans is lost, the individual human must acquire his value in some other way.[25]

Evaluation. The argument from decisive moments and the argument from gradualism both promote an agnostic position toward the beginning of life. Both argue that abortion should be legal because it is not possible to know when the unborn child achieves full humanness. This agnostic view, however, actually provides support for the pro-life position because if no one knows when full

---

[23] As quoted in Mary Jo Sharp, *Why I Still Believe: A Former Atheist's Reckoning with the Bad Reputation Christians Give a Good God* (Grand Rapids, MI: Zondervan, 2019), 188.

[24] Sharp, 189.

[25] Scott B. Rae, *Doing the Right Thing: Making Moral Choices in a World Full of Options* (Grand Rapids, MI: Zondervan, 2013), 94.

humanness is attained, then abortion may very well be the killing of a human person. As Beckwith writes, "Ignorance of a being's status is certainly not justification to kill it."[26]

Furthermore, there is good reason to think that full humanness begins at conception, as will be addressed later. Another problem with the agnostic claim is that many pro-choice proponents do actually take a position on when full humanness begins. For example, someone might argue that abortion should be permitted for the entire pregnancy. Can they then claim to not know the status of a human?[27]

In 1984, a British governmental committee called *Enquiry into Human Fertilization and Embryology* published *The Warnock Report*. This report failed to answer the question of when a human embryo becomes a person. The answer to that question is critical for deciding what research can be performed on an embryo. If the embryo possesses the rights of personhood, then it should not be put to death in the process of research. However, if the embryo is nothing more than a collection of living cells, then all types of research seem appropriate.[28]

---

[26] Beckwith, 92-93.

[27] Beckwith, 94.

[28] David John Atkinson, *Pastoral Ethics* (London: Lynx Communications, 1994), 197.

The Warnock Report initially admits that "the questions of when life or personhood begin appear to be questions of fact susceptible of straightforward answers," but it then goes on to say, "we hold that the answers to such questions in fact are complex amalgams of factual and moral judgments."[29] The report finally dodges the issue completely: "Instead of trying to answer these questions directly we have therefore gone straight to the question of how it is right to treat the human embryo."[30] That is an attempt to separate facts from values. However, such a separation is not possible. How can the writers of the report know how to treat an embryo (which is a question of values) if they do not have an answer to the question of when personhood begins (which is a question of fact)?[31]

This report strives to sever the link between medical facts and moral judgments. David John Atkinson writes that the report "operates with what we may call a 'socially defined concept of the human person' – and with a gradualist view of personal beginnings."[32] The report

---

[29] As quoted in Atkinson, 198.

[30] As quoted in Atkinson, 198.

[31] Atkinson, 200.

[32] Atkinson 201.

assigns a certain amount of status to the embryo. Yet, it does not grant to the embryo the rights of personhood. Personhood is presented as something into which the embryo must gradually grow, as an acorn must grow into an oak tree.[33]

The scientific evidence, which will be discussed in more detail later, clarifies that a human embryo is living, is human, and is a genetically distinct being. What is the result of living human beings not having the status of personhood?

As Atkinson points out, "Once we accept that there can be living human beings which are not protectable persons then someone has to decide when that protection is appropriate."[34] He goes on to write that "if protectable personhood is only socially defined, society could of course decide to define as non-protectable persons anyone that it found inconvenient."[35]

The performance and utilitarian views are both plagued by the futility of the attempt to make human value something that is measurable in degrees. Without sufficient consciousness to express a desire to live, a human could

---

[33] Atkinson 201.

[34] Atkinson, 201.

[35] Atkinson, 201.

be deemed as not possessing an adequate degree of personhood to deserve life. Tooley illustrates this: "I think that an entity cannot have a right to continued existence – or, indeed, any rights at all – unless it either has, or has had, conscious desires."[36]

Tooley's idea dismantles any notion of people possessing equal worth. Beckwith responds to that idea: "Intrinsic value is not a degreed property; you either have it or you don't."[37] Beyond that, who will decide which people have sufficient worth to deserve life? The potential ethical consequences should be readily apparent. As Myers asserts, "Equality is impossible if people are human by degrees." [38]

Some thinkers have created criteria for personhood. Mary Anne Warren developed a list of five traits: consciousness, reasoning, self-motivated activity, the capacity for communication, and the presence of self-concepts and self-awareness. In her view, someone must possess at least two of these traits to be considered a person.[39] These types of criteria are attempts to maintain a

---

[36]As quoted in Myers, 208.

[37]As quoted in Myers, 208.

[38] Myers, 209.

[39] Beckwith, 105-06.

distinction between humanness and personhood. One could reasonably wonder how Warren arrived at her list. Furthermore, how did she decide that meeting two criteria is a sufficient benchmark for personhood? Her reasoning appears to be arbitrary.

Singer's view makes human value dependent on cognitive capacity. It is indisputable that some humans have superior cognitive abilities than others. A person with advanced math skills would, in Singer's view, have greater worth and a greater right to life than someone who lacks those skills. His line of reasoning produces what could be called an "implicit caste system."[40]

Sharp explains that, in this view, a person could lose their personhood and the accompanying rights. If consciousness is made a criterion for personhood, "such a view leads to disastrous consequences, as humans lose consciousness when they fall asleep or fall into a coma. Every night billions of humans would lose their right to life based on normal human sleep patterns."[41]

This view leads to an absurd conclusion. Does human value really depend on consciousness? Someone who kills a sleeping person should undoubtedly be

---

[40] Sharp, 189.

[41] Sharp, 189.

considered guilty of taking a human life. The American Declaration of Independence states that humans are "endowed by their Creator with certain unalienable Rights."[42] This is the endowment view of human life: every human has been created with intrinsic value.[43]

A significant problem with any argument from criteria of personhood is how function is confused with being (or essence). Beckwith is unconvinced by the functional definitions of personhood. Functional definitions exclude not only the unborn but also those who are, for example, unconscious, sleeping, young, or dealing with intellectual disabilities. Beckwith asserts that "it seems more consistent with our moral intuitions to say that a person functions as a person because she is a person, not that she is a person because she functions as a person."[44]

A person can be functional, become nonfunctional (e.g., by going to sleep), and then return to a functional state. When a person goes through that cycle, they are regarded as the same person throughout. It is not thought that a new person has sprung into existence. It is reasonable to conclude that a person possesses an underlying personal

---

[42] As quoted in Myers, 207.

[43] Myers, 207.

[44] Beckwith, 108.

unity despite any changes in functionality they might experience.[45]

Beckwith refers to the SLED acronym, which was developed to describe the differences between the born and unborn. Those differences are size, level of development, environment, and degree of dependency. Both the decisive moment view and the gradualism view require accepting at least one of these differences as being morally relevant in the abortion debate.[46] However, Beckwith maintains that those are not ethically relevant distinctions. For example, in response to the environmental difference, Beckwith contends that "*Where* one is irrelevant to *who* one is."[47] The location of a child in its mother's womb does not diminish the value of the child.

Myers makes note of an essential implication of the SLED acronym when he writes that to assign human worth based on these criteria "is to say that those of us who are bigger, better developed, in a certain geographical location, and independent should have the right to determine the

---

[45] Beckwith, 108-09.

[46] Beckwith, 113-14.

[47] Beckwith, 114.

value of those who are less so."[48] He candidly declares, "This isn't something a Christian worldview can affirm."[49]

These four arguments (decisive moment, gradualism, performance, and utilitarianism) all have the potential to be arbitrary. The failures of these views support the position that personhood begins at conception.

The Commencement of Personhood

The critical issue in this discussion is the commencement of personhood. According to Myers, "The value of human life is a worldview issue drawing on philosophy, science, and theology. Human rights and moral values are at stake."[50] In light of that statement, further reflections will be offered regarding the commencement of personhood, alongside further critique of pro-abortion arguments.

Theological Considerations. Regarding abortion, John Stott describes how moral decisions hinge on what a human fetus is: "If 'it' were only a lump of jelly or blob of

---

[48] Myers, 214.

[49] Myers, 214.

[50] Myers, 204.

tissue, then of course it could be removed without qualms. But 'it' is actually a 'he' or 'she,' an unborn child."[51]

Stott appeals to Psalm 139, in which the psalmist reflects on his prenatal existence by focusing on several points. First, the psalmist refers to his creation. He considered himself to be the handiwork of a divine potter. Second, there is continuity in the psalmist's life. He surveyed his past (including his pre-birth state), present, and future. His use of *I* throughout the psalm indicates that he saw "a direct continuity between his antenatal and postnatal being."[52] From a biblical perspective, moments such as implantation or viability "are stages in the continuous process by which an individual human life is developing into mature human personhood."[53]

The Bible does not explicitly prohibit abortion, but numerous passages provide indirect condemnation:

- Genesis 1:26-27 (human life is sacred due to creation in the image of God)

---

[51] John Stott, "Cornerstone: Does Life Begin before Birth?," *Christianity Today* (Carol Stream, IL: Christianity Today, 1980), volume 24, number 15, 50.

[52] Stott, 50.

[53] Stott, 50.

- Exodus 21:22-25 (legal precedent supports the personhood of the unborn child);

- Leviticus 18:21 and Deuteronomy 12:31 (infanticide is condemned)

- Job 12:10 and Acts 17:25 (God is sovereign over life and death)

- Luke 1:41-44; 2:12-16 (the same Greek word is used to describe both an unborn child and a newborn infant).[54]

Karl Barth summarized the historic position of Christian theology on this issue when he wrote:

> [T]he unborn child is from the very first a child. It is still developing [. . .] But it is a man and not a thing, nor a mere part of the mother's body [. . .] he who destroys germinating life kills a man and thus ventures the monstrous thing of decreeing concerning the life and death of a fellow-man whose life is given by God.[55]

A substantial theological issue is what it means for humans to be created in the image of God. To define it

---

[54] C. Horn III and A. E. Hill, "Abortion," in Walter A. Elwell, *Evangelical Dictionary of Theology: Second Edition* (Grand Rapids, MI: Baker Academic, 2001), 16-17.

[55] Karl Barth, *Church Dogmatics: The Doctrine of Creation, Part 4*, volume 3, edited by Geoffrey William Bromiley and Thomas F. Torrance (Edinburgh: T&T Clark, 2004), 416.

simply, the image of God means that "There is something about the way God is that is like the way we are."[56]

Rebecca McLaughlin emphasizes the importance of acknowledging that humans are uniquely created by God:

> Our moral frameworks have been so inscribed with Christian valuing of the young and the weak that killing a baby feels horrific. But the logic is sound: if humans are not in a special category of personhood by virtue of their creation in the image of God, perhaps we should judge their value according to their capacities.[57]

Sam Storms defines *personhood* as "fundamentally a spiritual reality dependent upon the presence of the *image of God* in man."[58] As he cautions against any attempt to limit personhood, he clarifies that a merely functional definition of the image of God is inadequate: "The image of God is as much a *state* as it is a *capacity* [. . .] The image is a given, not a goal to which the fetus moves in its physiological development."[59]

---

[56] J. P. Moreland and Scott Rae, as quoted in Myers, 213.

[57] Rebecca McLaughlin, *Confronting Christianity: 12 Hard Questions for the World's Largest Religion* (Wheaton, IL: Crossway, 2019), 150.

[58] Sam Storms, *Christian Ethics* (Oklahoma City, OK: Sam Storms, 2006), 6.

[59] Storms, 7.

Storms goes on to say that the fetus' development is not a progression from non-person to full-person. Instead, the fetus develops from full personhood to a more complete expression of personhood.[60]

The concept of the image of God should be distinguished from speciesism, which is the secular term for when one species views itself as superior to another. Having been created in the image of God, humans are unique, but that does not give them the right to do whatever they wish to each other or the world around them.[61]

The image of God provides the foundation for human value. It also provides the foundation for human dignity because, as Beckwith clarifies, to be a human being is to be a particular type of substance, "even if it is not presently exhibiting the functions, behaving in [certain] ways, or currently able to immediately exercise these activities that we typically attribute to active and mature rational moral agents."[62]

The principle of continuity throughout life seems virtually indisputable. It would be unacceptable for a criminal to claim that his identity has been altered through

---

[60] Storms, 7.

[61] Myers, 213.

[62] As quoted in Myers, 214.

time and, therefore, he is not to be held responsible for a crime committed in the past. A person's cells are replaced over time, but that does not make her a different person. Beckwith explains, "Human beings [. . .] are ontologically prior to their parts, which means that the organism as a whole maintains absolute identity through time while it grows, develops, and undergoes numerous changes."[63]

The Old Testament addresses the image of God in Genesis 1:26-27, 5:1-3, and 9:6. Michael Heiser offers several observations about the image of God based on these passages. First, the image of God is gender-neutral. That means it applies to both males and females. Second, the image is a concept assigned only to humans. This phrase puts humanity in a unique category among created physical things.[64]

Third, in an observation that particularly challenges the pro-abortion arguments addressed earlier, "There is no hint that humanity grows into the image, or develops the image. There is no 'potential' image of God. Whatever the image of God means, it is by definition inseparable from the

---

[63] As quoted in Myers, 215.

[64] Michael S. Heiser, "Image of God," in *The Lexham Bible Dictionary*, edited by John D. Barry et al. (Bellingham, WA: Lexham Press, 2016), "Old Testament Data for the Image of God," Logos Research Edition.

human species."[65] Related to that is a fourth observation, which is that "Nothing suggests that the image has been or can be bestowed incrementally or partially. There is no 'partial' image."[66] Whatever the image of God is precisely, it is something that all humans share at all stages of their lives.

Scientific Considerations. The primary question concerns not when human life begins, although that is important, but rather when a human person becomes present. The most compelling explanation is the genetic view of personhood (also known as the biological or structural view). John S. Feinberg and Paul D. Feinberg summarize the genetic view by writing, "This is the view that when human life is present, there is a person with rights, one of which is the right to life."[67]

In this understanding, biological considerations establish personhood. One such consideration is the species-specific DNA strands that are present at the moment of conception. Those strands indicate the

---

[65] Heiser, "Old Testament Data for the Image of God."

[66] Heiser, "Old Testament Data for the Image of God."

[67] John S. Feinberg and Paul D. Feinberg, *Ethics for a Brave New World* (Wheaton, IL: Crossway Books, 1993), 60.

humanness of the fertilized egg. Therefore, abortion is immoral because personhood begins at conception.[68]

John MacArthur and Richard Mayhue point out:

Scientific fact demonstrates that human life begins at conception, when all twenty-three pairs of chromosomes are complete. The fertilized egg then contains a fixed genetic structure (DNA). Between days twelve and twenty-eight, a heart begins to beat. Blood cells form at day seventeen, and eyes begin to form at day nineteen. Between weeks four and six, brain waves can be measured. At one month, the embryo looks like a distinct human person. Fingerprints exist at two months. The skeleton, circulatory system, and muscular system are complete by the eighth week. The manifestation of personhood appears rapidly after conception.[69]

Ultrasound technology has significantly impacted the modern scientific understanding of pregnancy. It is reported that over seventy-five percent of the women who see an ultrasound image of their child at a pro-life pregnancy center decide against having an abortion.[70] The former abortion doctor Joseph Randall candidly admitted that he refused to show ultrasound images to the pregnant

---

[68] Feinberg and Feinberg, 60.

[69] John MacArthur and Richard Mayhue, eds., *Biblical Doctrine: A Systematic Summary of Bible Truth* (Wheaton, IL: Crossway, 2017), 433.

[70] Myers, 206.

women in his clinic "because we knew that if they so much as heard the heart beat, they wouldn't want to have an abortion."[71]

Understanding prenatal development from a scientific perspective is essential for countering the idea that the unborn are not fully human. Pregnancy begins at the moment of conception when the male sperm and the female ovum unite. The zygote results from fertilization and is biologically alive, as demonstrated by the fact that it possesses the four criteria for life: metabolism, growth, reaction to stimuli, and reproduction. The humanness of the zygote is indisputable because the zygote is the product of human parents. The zygote is a unique individual with its own genetic code. All the genetic information (including characteristics such as gender and hair color) that the child will ever have during his entire life is already present. The whole person is there in a tiny form.[72]

Eckman clarifies that "there is substantial identity between the embryo, the viable fetus, the infant, the child, the adult, and the elderly person. The fetus is a person."[73] According to biophysicist Francis Crick, the genetic content

---

[71] As quoted in Myers, 206.

[72] Beckwith, 42.

[73] Eckman, 30.

in a newly fertilized ovum possesses the same quantity of information as fifty complete sets of the *Encyclopedia Brittanica.*[74]

The terms *zygote, embryo,* and *fetus* refer to stages in a person's development. It is more accurate to assert, for example, that someone once was a fetus than to argue, as pro-abortionists do, that someone came from a fetus.[75] Adolescence is also a stage in a person's development, but who would say that an adult came from an adolescent? Instead, it would be declared that the adult was once an adolescent.

There are four scientific reasons why the unborn should be regarded as fully human. First, at conception, the child possesses its own unique genetic code. Second, "The conceptus is a being who is in the process of becoming."[76] That statement differs significantly from thinking of the conceptus as a *becoming* striving toward *being.* Third, the conceptus results from the union of its human parents. Finally, there is continuity in the development of the zygote

---

[74] Norman Geisler and Frank Turek, *Legislating Morality: Is It Wise? Is It Legal? Is It Possible?* (Eugene, OR: Wipf and Stock Publishers, 2003), 155.

[75] Beckwith, 43.

[76] Beckwith, 45.

throughout its life into adulthood. The human entity begins at conception and never becomes a different individual.[77]

Because the fertilized ovum possesses all of the genetic information the person will ever have, it does not make sense to regard the unborn child as only a potential person.[78] "Rather, it is a life with great potential."[79]

Responses to Objections. Several objections could be directed toward the genetic view of personhood. One objection is the claim that grounding personhood in the genetic code means that personhood is reduced to nothing more than chemical values. In response, it could be highlighted that the primary focus should be on the specific combination of chemicals found in humans. Other standards of determining personhood have the potential to be arbitrary and subjective. By contrast, the genetic code provides an objective basis for determining personhood.[80]

This distinctive genetic code makes each individual unique. Every person is unlike any other creature ever

---

[77] Beckwith, 45.

[78] Beckwith, 117.

[79] Geisler and Turek, 156.

[80] Feinberg and Feinberg, 60-61.

conceived. It also makes them one hundred percent human.[81]

A more substantial objection pertains to twinning and mosaics. In twinning, the developing zygote splits into two zygotes. Since this happens between seven and fourteen days after conception, how could it be said that there is a person at conception who then becomes two persons? A similar problem is posed by mosaics, which is when two eggs are fertilized, but only one is absorbed and subsequently born. Both of these examples have been taken to suggest that there is some fluidity regarding personhood in the early days of life.[82]

Feinberg and Feinberg respond by writing, "Check the DNA strands. They are species-specific at the point of conception. The most that is demonstrated by this argument is that until after blastocyst we do not know *how many* persons are present, but that is clearly a different question than whether personhood is present."[83]

Ethical Implications. Four conditions are required for an action to be considered murder: "1. A person must be killed. 2. The person must be killed intentionally. 3. The

---

[81] Geisler and Turek, 155.

[82] Feinberg and Feinberg, 61.

[83] Feinberg and Feinberg, 62.

victim must be innocent. 4. An unlawful or sinful motive must be involved in the killing."[84] It could reasonably be concluded that "Abortion as commonly practiced today satisfies these criteria."[85] "Personhood is not a development; it is an event."[86] To further clarify the ethical implications of this issue, MacArthur and Mayhue write:

> Attempts to separate personhood from biological human life are unscientific, arbitrary, and dangerous. All that physically constitutes a person is made immediately at conception. Biological human life means that personhood exists. A human life is a person. Separating human life from personhood has resulted in the killing of persons in the womb through abortion and has even led to the murder of babies after birth.[87]

Conclusion

McLaughlin writes that an essential aspect of the Christian worldview is "the recognition that unborn babies are fully human and therefore infinitely valuable."[88] That makes every individual a part of "a much larger story, a

---

[84] MacArthur and Mayhue, 434-35.

[85] MacArthur and Mayhue, 435.

[86] MacArthur and Mayhue, 434.

[87] MacArthur and Mayhue, 434.

[88] McLaughlin, 152.

story in which the most vulnerable are the most important, a story in which no human being is unwanted."[89]

The case for the humanity and personhood of the unborn can be made by demonstrating the inadequacy of pro-abortion arguments and by appealing to appropriate theological, scientific, and ethical considerations. Not only are there no persuasive reasons to distinguish between humanness and personhood, but there are also compelling reasons to affirm that all who possess human life also possess full personhood and should, therefore, be treated as valuable human persons.

---

[89] McLaughlin, 152.

Discussion Starters

1. What surprised you regarding the debates surrounding humanness and personhood?

2. Have you ever encountered any abortion-rights arguments? If so, were you able to offer a meaningful response? How would you respond now?

3. What are the theological implications of humanity's creation in the image of God?

4. What are the ethical implications of this content?

Bibliography

Ali, Abdullah Yusuf, translator. *The Meaning of the Holy Qur'an.* Bellingham, WA: Logos Bible Software Research Edition, 2004.

Arndt, William, Frederick W. Danker, and Walter Bauer. *A Greek-English Lexicon of the New Testament and Other Early Christian Literature.* Chicago: University of Chicago Press, 2000.

Atkinson, David John. *Pastoral Ethics.* London: Lynx Communications, 1994.

Bahnsen, Greg L. *Presuppositional Apologetics: Stated and Defended.* Edited by Joel McDurmon. Powder Springs, GA; Nacogdoches, TX: American Vision; Covenant Media Press, 2008.

Barnett, Tim. "Why Apologetics?" Stand to Reason. Published December 26, 2018. Accessed April 2, 2024. https://www.str.org/w/why-apologetics-.

Barth, Karl. *Church Dogmatics: The Doctrine of Creation, Part 4.* Volume 3. Edited by Geoffrey William Bromiley and Thomas F. Torrance. Edinburgh: T&T Clark, 2004.

Beckwith, Francis J. *Politically Correct Death: Answering Arguments for Abortion Rights.* Grand Rapids, MI: Baker Books, 1993.

Beckwith, Francis J., and Gregory Koukl. *Relativism: Feet Firmly Planted in Mid-Air.* Grand Rapids, MI: Baker Books, 1998.

Beilby, James K. "Varieties of Apologetics." Edited by Khaldoun A. Sweis and Chad V. Meister. *Christian Apologetics: An Anthology of Primary Sources.* Grand Rapids, MI: Zondervan, 2012.

Boa, Kenneth, and Robert M. Bowman Jr. *Faith Has Its Reasons: Integrative Approaches to Defending the Christian Faith.* Westmont, IL: IVP Books, 2012.

Boice, James Montgomery. *Acts: An Expositional Commentary.* Grand Rapids, MI: Baker Books, 1997.

Brierley, Justin. *The Surprising Rebirth of Belief in God: Why New Atheism Grew Old and Secular Thinkers Are Considering Christianity Again.* Carol Stream, IL: Tyndale Elevate, 2023.

Clark, David K. *Dialogical Apologetics: A Person-Centered Approach to Christian Defense.* Grand Rapids, MI: Baker Books, 1993.

Copan, Paul. *"True for You but Not for Me."* Minneapolis, MN: Bethany House, 2009.

Cottrell, Jack. *The Faith Once for All: Bible Doctrine for Today.* Joplin, MO: College Press Publishing Company, 2002.

Courson, Jon. *Jon Courson's Application Commentary.* Nashville, TN: Thomas Nelson, 2003.

Cowan, Steven B., and James S. Spiegel. *The Love of Wisdom: A Christian Introduction to Philosophy.* Nashville, TN: B&H Academic, 2009.

Craig, William Lane. *On Guard: Defending Your Faith with Reason and Precision.* Colorado Springs, CO: David C Cook, 2010.

_____. *Reasonable Faith: Christian Truth and Apologetics.* Revised edition. Wheaton, IL: Crossway Books, 1994.

Dennis, J. "Death of Jesus." Edited by Joel B. Green, Jeannine K. Brown, and Nicholas Perrin. *Dictionary of Jesus and the Gospels, Second Edition.* Downers Grove, IL; Nottingham, England: IVP Academic, 2013.

Douma, Doug J. *The Presbyterian Philosopher: The Authorized Biography of Gordon H. Clark.* Eugene, OR: Wipf and Stock, 2016.

Eckman, James P. *Biblical Ethics: Choosing Right in a World Gone Wrong.* Biblical Essentials Series. Wheaton, IL: Crossway Books, 2004.

Evans, C. A. "Jesus in Non-Christian Sources." Edited by Joel B. Green and Scot McKnight. *Dictionary of Jesus and the Gospels.* Downers Grove, IL: InterVarsity Press, 1992.

Evans, C. Stephen. *Pocket Dictionary of Apologetics & Philosophy of Religion.* Downers Grove, IL: InterVarsity Press, 2002.

Feinberg, John S., and Paul D. Feinberg. *Ethics for a Brave New World.* Wheaton, IL: Crossway Books, 1993.

Fernandes, Phil. *The Fernandes Guide to Apologetic Methodologies.* Ottawa, ON: True Freedom Press, 2024.

Foulkes, Francis. "Death of Christ." Edited by Walter A. Elwell. *Evangelical Dictionary of Biblical Theology.* Baker Reference Library. Grand Rapids, MI: Baker Book House, 1996.

Frame, John M. "Presuppositional Apologetics." Edited by Stanley N. Gundry and Steven B. Cowan. *Five Views on Apologetics*. Zondervan Counterpoints Collection. Grand Rapids, MI: Zondervan, 2000.

Gangel, Kenneth O. *Acts*. Volume 5. Holman New Testament Commentary. Nashville, TN: Broadman & Holman, 1998.

Gardner, H. Lynn. *Commending and Defending Christian Faith: An Introduction to Christian Apologetics*. Joplin, MO: College Press Publishing Company, 2010.

Garrett, James Leo, Jr. *Systematic Theology: Biblical, Historical, and Evangelical*. Second edition. Volume 2. Eugene, OR: Wipf & Stock, 2014.

Geisler, David. "What is Conversational Apologetics?" Edited by Joseph M. Holden. *The Comprehensive Guide to Apologetics*. Eugene, OR: Harvest House, 2024.

Geisler, David, and Norman Geisler. *Conversational Apologetics: Connecting with People to Share Jesus*. Eugene, OR: Harvest House Publishers, 2014.

Geisler, Norman L. *Baker Encyclopedia of Christian Apologetics*. Baker Reference Library. Grand Rapids, MI: Baker Books, 1999.

_____. *Christian Apologetics*. Grand Rapids, MI: Baker Book House, 1976.

_____. *The Battle for the Resurrection*. Eugene, OR: Wipf & Stock Publishers, 1992.

Geisler, Norman L., and Ronald M. Brooks. *When Skeptics Ask: A Handbook on Christian Evidences*. Revised and updated. Grand Rapids, MI: Baker Books, 2013.

Geisler, Norman L., and Paul D. Feinberg. *Introduction to Philosophy: A Christian Perspective.* Grand Rapids, MI: Baker Book House, 1980.

Geisler, Norman L., and Abdul Saleeb. *Answering Islam: The Crescent in Light of the Cross.* Second edition. Grand Rapids, MI: Baker Books, 2002.

Geisler, Norman, and Frank Turek. *Legislating Morality: Is It Wise? Is It Legal? Is It Possible?* Eugene, OR: Wipf and Stock Publishers, 2003.

Geisler, Norman L., and William D. Watkins. *Worlds Apart: A Handbook on World Views.* Second edition. Grand Rapids, MI: Baker Book House, 1989.

Green, J. B. "Death of Christ." Edited by Gerald F. Hawthorne, Ralph P. Martin, and Daniel G. Reid. *Dictionary of Paul and His Letters.* Downers Grove, IL: InterVarsity Press, 1993.

_____. "Death of Jesus." Edited by Scot McKnight. *Dictionary of Jesus and the Gospels.* Downers Grove, IL: InterVarsity Press, 1992.

Groothuis, Douglas. *Christian Apologetics: A Comprehensive Case for Biblical Faith.* Downers Grove, IL; Nottingham, England: IVP Academic; Apollos, 2011.

Habermas, Gary R. "Evidential Apologetics." Edited by Stanley N. Gundry and Steven B. Cowan. *Five Views on Apologetics.* Zondervan Counterpoints Collection. Grand Rapids, MI: Zondervan, 2000.

_____. *The Historical Jesus: Ancient Evidence for the Life of Christ.* Joplin, MO: College Press Publishing Company, 1996.

Harris, W. Hall, III, Elliot Ritzema, Rick Brannan, Douglas Mangum, John Dunham, Jeffrey A. Reimer, and Micah Wierenga, eds. *The Lexham English Bible.* Bellingham, WA: Lexham Press, 2013.

Heiser, Michael S. "Image of God." Edited by John D. Barry, David Bomar, Derek R. Brown, Rachel Klippenstein, Douglas Mangum, Carrie Sinclair Wolcott, Lazarus Wentz, Elliot Ritzema, and Wendy Widder. *The Lexham Bible Dictionary.* Bellingham, WA: Lexham Press, 2016.

Horn III, C., and A. E. Hill. "Abortion." Edited by Walter A. Elwell. *Evangelical Dictionary of Theology: Second Edition.* Grand Rapids, MI: Baker Academic, 2001.

Hughes, R. Kent. *Mark: Jesus, Servant and Savior.* Preaching the Word. Westchester, IL: Crossway Books, 1989.

Janosik, Daniel. *The Guide to Answering Islam: What Every Christian Needs to Know about Islam and the Rise of Radical Islam.* Cambridge, OH: Christian Publishing House, 2019.

Köstenberger, Andreas J. *John.* Baker Exegetical Commentary on the New Testament. Grand Rapids, MI: Baker Academic, 2004.

Koukl, Gregory. *Street Smarts: Using Questions to Answer Christianity's Toughest Challenges.* Grand Rapids, MI: Zondervan Reflective, 2023.

_____. *Tactics, 10th Anniversary Edition: A Game Plan for Discussing Your Christian Convictions.* Grand Rapids, MI: Zondervan, 2019.

Kreeft, Peter, and Ronald K. Tacelli. *Handbook of Christian Apologetics: Hundreds of Answers to Crucial Questions.* Westmont, IL: IVP Academic, 1994.

Leventhal, Barry R. "Why I Believe Jesus Is the Promised Messiah." In *Why I Am a Christian: Leading Thinkers Explain Why They Believe.* Grand Rapids, MI: Baker Books, 2001.

Lewis, C. S. *Mere Christianity.* New York: HarperOne, 2001.

_____. *The Weight of Glory: And Other Addresses.* New York: HarperOne, 2001.

Lisle, Jason. *The Ultimate Proof of Creation: Resolving the Origins Debate.* Green Forest, AR: Master Books, 2009.

MacArthur, John, and Richard Mayhue, eds. *Biblical Doctrine: A Systematic Summary of Bible Truth.* Wheaton, IL: Crossway, 2017.

Martin, Walter. *The Kingdom of the Cults: The Definitive Work on the Subject.* Grand Rapids, MI: Bethany House, 2019.

McDowell, Josh, and Sean McDowell. *Evidence That Demands a Verdict: Life-Changing Truth for a Skeptical World.* Nashville, TN: Thomas Nelson, 2017.

_____. *More Than a Carpenter.* Revised edition. Carol Stream, IL: Tyndale Momentum, 2009.

McFarland, Alex. *10 Answers for Atheists: How to Have an Intelligent Discussion about the Existence of God.* Bloomington, MN: Bethany House, 2012.

McGrath, Alister E. *Mere Apologetics: How to Help Seekers and Skeptics Find Faith.* Grand Rapids, MI: Baker Books, 2012.

McLaughlin, Rebecca. *Confronting Christianity: 12 Hard Questions for the World's Largest Religion.* Wheaton, IL: Crossway, 2019.

Morgan, Garry R. *Understanding World Religions in 15 Minutes a Day.* Minneapolis, MN: Bethany House Publishers, 2012.

Myers, Jeff. *Understanding the Culture: A Survey of Social Engagement.* Manitou Springs, CO: Summit Ministries, 2017.

Myers, Jeff, and David A. Noebel. *Understanding the Times: A Survey of Competing Worldviews.* Manitou Springs, CO: Summit Ministries, 2015.

Newman, Randy. *Questioning Evangelism: Engaging People's Hearts the Way Jesus Did.* Grand Rapids, MI: Kregel Publications, 2004.

Newman, Randy, and Joel S. Woodruff. *Conversational Apologetics Course: Practicing the Art of Sharing Your Faith with Others.* Springfield, VA: C.S. Lewis Institute, 2014.

Obitts, S. R. "Philosophy, Christian View Of." Edited by Walter A. Elwell. *Evangelical Dictionary of Theology: Second Edition.* Grand Rapids, MI: Baker Academic, 2001.

Pearcey, Nancy. "Foreword." In Gregory Koukl, *The Story of Reality: How the World Began, How It Ends, and Everything Important That Happens in Between.* Grand Rapids, MI: Zondervan, 2017.

Phillips, Timothy R., and Dennis L. Okholm. *Christian Apologetics in the Postmodern World.* Downers Grove, IL: InterVarsity Press, 1995.

Pinnock, Clark H. "Apologetics." Edited by Sinclair B. Ferguson and J. I. Packer. *New Dictionary of Theology*. Downers Grove, IL: InterVarsity Press, 2000.

Powell, Doug. *Holman QuickSource Guide to Christian Apologetics*. Nashville, TN: Holman Reference, 2006.

Poythress, Vern S. "Why Philosophy Matters for Christians." Crossway. Published October 7, 2014. Accessed March 25, 2024. https://www.crossway.org/articles/why-philosophy-matters-for-christians/.

Prigodich, Raymond. "Pre-evangelism." Edited by A. Scott Moreau, Harold Netland, and Charles van Engen. *Evangelical Dictionary of World Missions*. Grand Rapids, MI: Baker Reference Library, 2000.

Qureshi, Nabeel. *Answering Jihad: A Better Way Forward*. Grand Rapids, MI: Zondervan, 2016.

_____. *No God but One: Allah or Jesus?* Grand Rapids, MI: Zondervan, 2016.

Rae, Scott B. *Doing the Right Thing: Making Moral Choices in a World Full of Options*. Grand Rapids, MI: Zondervan, 2013.

Roth, Amanda. "When does the fetus acquire a moral status of a human being? The philosophy of 'gradualism' can provide answers." The Conversation. Published June 30, 2022. Accessed April 24, 2024. https://theconversation.com/when-does-the-fetus-acquire-a-moral-status-of-a-human-being-the-philosophy-of-gradualism-can-provide-answers-185938.

Sharp, Mary Jo. *Why I Still Believe: A Former Atheist's Reckoning with the Bad Reputation Christians Give a Good God*. Grand Rapids, MI: Zondervan, 2019.

Shumack, Richard. *The Wisdom of Islam and the Foolishness of Christianity: A Christian Response to Nine Objections to Christianity by Muslim Philosophers.* Sydney, Australia: Island View Publishing, 2014.

Smith, Wilbur M. *Therefore Stand.* New Canaan, CT: Keats Publishing, 1981.

Soanes, Catherine, and Angus Stevenson, eds. *Concise Oxford English Dictionary.* Oxford: Oxford University Press, 2004.

Spurgeon, Charles H. "The Wedding Was Furnished with Guests." In *The Metropolitan Tabernacle Pulpit Sermons,* 34:253-264. London: Passmore & Alabaster, 1888.

Stafford, Tim. "Church in Action: Hugh Ross's Apologetics Hot Line." *Christianity Today.* Volume 35. Number 3. Carol Stream, IL: Christianity Today, 1991.

Storms, Sam. *Christian Ethics.* Oklahoma City, OK: Sam Storms, 2006.

Story, Dan. *Christianity on the Offense: Responding to the Beliefs and Assumptions of Spiritual Seekers.* Grand Rapids, MI: Kregel Publications, 1998.

_____. *Engaging the Closed Minded: Presenting Your Faith to the Confirmed Unbeliever.* Grand Rapids, MI: Kregel Publications, 1999.

Stott, John. "Cornerstone: Does Life Begin before Birth?" *Christianity Today.* Volume 24. Number 15. Carol Stream, IL: Christianity Today, 1980.

_____. *The Preacher's Notebook: The Collected Quotes, Illustrations, and Prayers of John Stott.* Edited by Mark Meynell. Bellingham, WA: Lexham Press, 2018.

Strobel, Lee. *The Case for Christianity Answer Book.* Grand Rapids, MI: Zondervan, 2014.

_____. *The Case for Faith: A Journalist Investigates the Toughest Objections to Christianity.* Grand Rapids, MI: Zondervan, 2000.

Turek, Frank. *Stealing from God: Why Atheists Need God to Make Their Case.* Colorado Springs, CO: NavPress, 2014.

Van Til, Cornelius. *Christian Apologetics.* Edited by William Edgar. Second edition. P&R Publishing Company: Phillipsburg, NJ, 2003.

White, James R. *What Every Christian Needs to Know about the Qur'an.* Minneapolis, MN: Bethany House Publishers, 2013.

Wiersbe, Warren W. *The Bible Exposition Commentary.* Wheaton, IL: Victor Books, 1996.

Wise, Kurt P. *Faith, Form, and Time: What the Bible Teaches and Science Confirms about Creation and the Age of the Universe.* Nashville, TN: Broadman & Holman, 2002.